# GREAT
# AMERICAN
# CONSPIRACIES

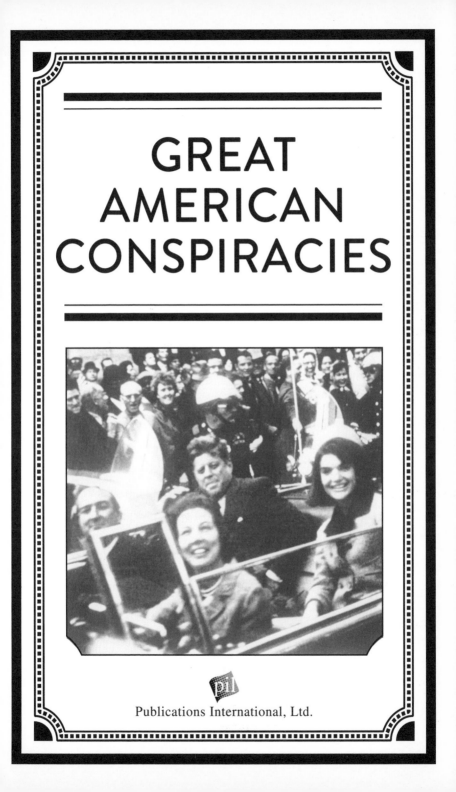

Publications International, Ltd.

**CONTRIBUTING WRITERS:** A. L. Avila, Jeff Bahr, Fiona Broome, Jim Daley, Tom DeMichael, Katherine Don, James Duplacey, Eric Ethier, Ian Feigle, David Gerardi, Peter Haugen, Jonathan Kelley, Shanon Lyon, Patricia Martinelli, Paul Morie, David Morrow, Richard Mueller, Robert Norris, J.R. Raphael, Russ Roberts, Lawrence Robinson, Lexi M. Schuh, Paul Seaburn, Beth Taylor, Don Vaughan, Amanda Wegner, Jennifer Plattner Wilkinson, James Willis, and Kelly Wittmann

**COVER ART:** Library of Congress
**INTERIOR ART:** Art Explosion, Clipart.com, Getty, Library of Congress, Shutterstock.com, and Wikimedia Commons

Louis Weber, CEO
Publications International, Ltd.
8140 Lehigh Avenue
Morton Grove, IL 60053

ISBN: 978-1-64030-209-9

Manufactured in China.

8  7  6  5  4  3  2  1

# TABLE OF CONTENTS

# TEAPOT DOME SCANDAL

The Teapot Dome Scandal was the largest of numerous scandals during the presidency of Warren Harding. Teapot Dome is an oil field reserved for emergency use by the U.S. Navy located on public land in Wyoming. Oil companies and politicians claimed the reserves were not necessary and that the oil companies could supply the navy in the event of shortages. In 1922, Interior Secretary Albert B. Fall accepted $404,000 in illegal gifts from oil company executives in return for leasing the rights to the oil at Teapot Dome to Mammoth Oil without asking for competitive bids. The leases were legal but the gifts were not. Fall's attempts to keep the gifts secret failed, and, on April 14, 1922, *The Wall Street Journal* exposed the bribes. Fall denied the charges, but an investigation revealed a $100,000 no-interest loan in return for leases that Fall had forgotten to cover up. In 1927, the Supreme Court ruled that the oil leases had been illegally obtained, and the U.S. Navy regained control of Teapot Dome and other reserves. Fall was found guilty of bribery in 1929, fined $100,000, and sentenced to one year in prison. He was the first cabinet member imprisoned for his actions while in office. President Harding was not aware of the scandal at the time of his death in 1923, but it contributed to his administration being considered one of the most corrupt in history.

# THE PLOT TO ASSASSINATE PRESIDENT TRUMAN

Puerto Ricans have sought independence from the United States for decades. In 1950, two ardent nationalists took matters into their own hands as part of a campaign to win independence through violent means. Their target? President Harry Truman.

Members of the Puerto Rican Nationalist Party were spoiling for a fight. They had tried—and failed—to reach their goal of independence through electoral participation. By the 1930s, party leader Dr. Pedro Albuzu Campos was advocating a campaign of violent revolution. Throughout the 1930s and 1940s, the Nationalist Party was involved in one confrontation after another. In 1936, Albuzu was charged with conspiring to overthrow the government and was incarcerated. He spent the next six years in jail in New York. When he finally returned to Puerto Rico in 1947, the tinder of *nacionalismo puertorriqueño* was bone-dry and smoldering.

## THE MATCH IS LIT

On October 30, 1950, nationalists seized the town of Jayuya. With air support, the Puerto Rico National Guard crushed the rebellion. Griselio Torresola and Oscar Collazo, two nacionalistas, decided to retaliate at the highest level— the president of the United States.

They had help from natural wastage. The White House, which looks majestic from the outside, has been quite the wretched dump at many points in its history. By 1948, it was physically unsound, so the Truman family moved to Blair House. It would be a lot easier to whack a president there than it would have been at the White House.

## THE ATTEMPT

At 2:20 P.M. on November 1, 1950, Torresola approached the Pennsylvania Avenue entrance from the west with a 9mm Luger pistol. Collazo came from the east carrying the Luger's cheaper successor, the Walther P38. White House police guarded the entrance. Truman was upstairs taking a nap.

Collazo approached the Blair House steps, facing the turned back of Officer Donald Birdzell, and fired, shattering Birdzell's knee. Nearby Officers Floyd Boring and Joseph Davidson fired at Collazo through a wrought-iron fence but without immediate effect. Birdzell dragged himself after Collazo, firing his pistol. Then bullets from Boring and Davidson grazed Collazo in the scalp and chest—seemingly minor wounds. Out of ammo, Collazo sat down to reload his weapon.

Officer Leslie Coffelt staffed a guard booth at the west corner as Torresola took him unaware. Coffelt fell with a chest full of holes. Next, Torresola fired on Officer Joseph Downs, who had just stopped to chat with Coffelt. Downs took bullets to the hip, then the back and neck. He staggered to the basement door and locked it, hoping to deny the assassins entry. Torresola advanced on Birdzell from behind as the officer engaged Collazo and fired, hitting his other knee. Birdzell lost consciousness as Torresola reloaded.

Weapon recharged, Oscar Collazo stood, and then collapsed from his wounds. At that moment, a startled Truman came to the window to see what was the matter. Torresola was 31 feet away. If he had looked up at precisely the right moment, the Puerto Rican nationalist would have achieved his mission.

Officer Coffelt had one final police duty in life. Despite three chest wounds, he forced himself to his feet, took careful aim, and fired. A bullet splattered the brain matter of Griselio Torresola all over the street. Coffelt staggered back to the guard shack and crumpled.

Collazo survived and was sentenced to death. Before leaving office, President Truman commuted Collazo's sentence to life imprisonment.

Officers Downs and Birdzell recovered. Officer Leslie Coffelt died four hours later. The Secret Service's day room at Blair House is now named the Leslie W. Coffelt Memorial Room.

# THE BURR CONSPIRACY

Forget Hollywood: One of America's most dramatic plotlines comes straight from the Buckeye State. The scene involves a deadly duel, an island-based militia, and a plot to take over multiple states—all at the hands of a former vice president.

Aaron Burr gained fame as vice president under Thomas Jefferson from 1801 to 1805. It was toward the end of that term, though, that Burr's name really became notorious.

In July 1804, Burr decided he'd heard enough slandering from his political opponent, Alexander Hamilton. Burr and Hamilton, who was once the secretary of the Treasury, faced off in a historic duel at Weehawken, New Jersey. Burr won, shooting and killing Hamilton. (The partisan infighting of today's politics clearly pales in comparison to that of yesteryear's.)

Needless to say, the whole idea of murdering a political opponent didn't go over so well in Washington. Burr still finished his term as VP but soon headed west to carry out some more sinister plans. In those days, the West was wild, with sparse settlements and limited control. Burr had his sights set on the newly acquired Louisiana Purchase along with the future great state of Texas, which was still colonized by Spain. Burr figured he might as well build his own military, dominate the land, and establish his own empire.

## BURR FINDS A FELLOW CONSPIRATOR

Burr's first brainstorm was to turn to Britain. The inspired conspirator met with the nation's U.S. minister and threw out the idea of leading a revolt in the West in exchange for his country's money and ships. The boys from Britain, however, weren't too keen on the concept, and the plan never came together.

Still, Burr was determined. In 1806, he secured the support of a wealthy Irish American by the name of Harman Blennerhassett. Blennerhassett owned his own island, a small spread in the Ohio River now known as Blennerhassett Island. Burr and Blennerhassett teamed up on a mission to take over the world—or at least take over part of America. The two started stockpiling military supplies and training a militia on the private island. A U.S. Army commander named James Wilkinson was kind enough to provide them with heavy artillery.

Just when Burr's grand conspiracy really seemed to be shaping up, his plans took a turn for the worse. Newspapers started picking up word of the army he was creating. It wasn't until the governor of Ohio stepped in, though, that the joyride really came to an end.

Ohio's state militia raided Blennerhassett Island. The troops took boats and supplies, but Burr, Blennerhassett, and most of their army were already long gone.

## THE FALLOUT

Burr could only hide for so long. By early 1807, Burr was captured and put on trial. The case, heard by the Supreme Court, would become one of history's most famous. The evidence made it clear that Burr had toyed with the idea of building his own military in the West. Burr, though, argued that the Constitution defined true treason as an overt—not merely planned—military act. What's more, he said the act had to take place in the same district where the case was being tried.

All that legal gobbledygook ended up meaning a lot: Burr, his crew admitted, did deal with a militia and enough weapons to weigh down a herd of elephants while in Ohio. But, no one could prove that any of it was actually intended to be used for treason—and no one could definitively connect the material items with the bad guy pep talks Burr had given to his followers. Given all that, the judge ended up ruling in Burr's favor.

It probably goes without saying that the case brought a lot of attention to the state. Ohioans took great pride in their governor's fast action in invading Blennerhassett Island and stopping a potential disaster. Still, sometimes it's best to leave a tainted past behind. Ohio ended up saying so long to Blennerhassett Island, giving it to West Virginia and cutting its ties with the troubling land.

# WATERGATE

Watergate is the name of the scandal that caused Richard Nixon to become the only U.S. president to resign from office. On May 27, 1972, concerned that Nixon's bid for reelection was in jeopardy, former CIA agent E. Howard Hunt Jr., former New York assistant district attorney G. Gordon Liddy, former CIA operative James W. McCord Jr., and six other men broke into the Democratic headquarters in the Watergate Hotel in Washington, D.C. They wiretapped phones, stole some documents, and photographed others. When they broke in again on June 17 to fix a bug that wasn't working, a suspicious security guard called the Washington police, who arrested McCord and four other burglars. A cover-up began to destroy incriminating evidence, obstruct investigations, and halt any spread of scandal that might lead to the president. On August 29, Nixon announced that the break-in had been investigated and that no one in the White House was involved. Despite his efforts to hide his involvement, Nixon was done in by his own tape recordings, one of which revealed that he had authorized hush money paid to Hunt. To avoid impeachment, Nixon resigned on August 9, 1974. His successor, President Gerald Ford, granted him a blanket pardon on September 8, 1974, eliminating any possibility that Nixon would be indicted and tried. *Washington Post* reporters Bob Woodward and Carl Bernstein helped expose the scandal using information leaked by someone identified as Deep Throat, a source whose identity was kept hidden until 2005, when it was revealed that Deep Throat was former Nixon administration member William Mark Felt.

# BARACK OBAMA CITIZENSHIP CONSPIRACY THEORIES

During Barack Obama's 2008 presidential campaign and throughout his presidency, a number of conspiracy theories falsely asserted that Obama was not a natural-born citizen of the United States and was thus constitutionally unqualified to hold the office. Theories promoted by "birthers" alleged that Obama's published birth certificate was a forgery; that his actual birthplace was Kenya (not Hawaii); that Obama became a citizen of Indonesia in childhood, thereby losing his U.S. citizenship; and that Obama was not a natural-born U.S. citizen because he was born a dual British and American citizen.

Despite Obama's release of his official Hawaiian birth certificate in 2008, confirmation by the Hawaii Department of Health based on the original documents, the April 2011 release of a certified copy of Obama's original Certificate of Live Birth (long-form birth certificate), and birth announcements published in Hawaii newspapers, some people continue to doubt Obama's U.S. birth.

### CLAIM:

A Certified Registration of Birth issued in Kenya documents that Barack Obama was born in Mombasa, Kenya.

### FACT:

On August 2, 2009, Dr. Orly Taitz released a photograph of a document purporting to be a Certified Copy of Registration of Birth issued by the Republic of Kenya in February 1964, which recorded a "Barack Hussein II" as having been born in Mombasa, Kenya, in August 1961. The document is dated February 17, 1964, and purports to have been issued by the "Republic of Kenya." But Kenya (a former British colony) didn't officially adopt that name until December 12, 1964. In February 1964, it was known as the Dominion of Kenya. Additionally, Mombasa, originally part of Zanzibar, wasn't incorporated into Kenya until the latter became an independent nation in 1963, two years after Obama was born.

## CLAIM:

Obama obtained Indonesian citizenship (and thus may have lost U.S. citizenship) when he lived there as a child.

## FACT:

As an attempt to prove that Obama was no longer a U.S. citizen (or held dual citizenship), some claim his trip to Pakistan in 1981 took place at a time when there was supposedly a ban on United States passport holders entering that country, which would in turn have required him to use a non-U.S. passport. There was in fact no such ban. A *New York Times* article and U.S. State Department travel advisories from 1981 make it clear that travel to Pakistan by U.S. passport holders was legal at that time.

# IS OBAMA A SECRET MUSLIM?

Although Barack Obama is Christian, polls and surveys have shown that a number of Americans believe he is secretly a Muslim.

## CLAIM:

Barack Obama took the oath of office for the U.S. Senate in 2005 on a Qur'an rather than a Bible.

## FACT:

Obama was sworn into office for the U.S. Senate using a Bible that he owned. Two press reports from Obama's 2005 swearing-in ceremony specifically mention that Obama took the oath of office on his own copy of the Bible. This false claim may have been inspired by the 2007 swearing-in of the first Muslim elected to Congress, Representative Keith Ellison, who used a Qur'an that once belonged to Thomas Jefferson.

## CLAIM:

Barack Obama spent four years educated in a radical Muslim school know as a madrassa in Indonesia.

## FACT:

Obama attended two schools during the four years he lived in Indonesia as a child. He attended the Roman Catholic St. Francis Assisi School. Obama also attended State Elementary School Menteng 01, also known as Besuki School. Besuki is a public school.

While Obama's registration form indicates his religion was Muslim, there are errors on the forms and it seems reasonable to assume that he was registered as Muslim simply because his stepfather was nominally Muslim. Investigations by CNN, the Associated Press, the *Los Angeles Times,* and the *Chicago Tribune* found that Besuki School was a public school where students wore Western clothing and prayer was a small part of the curriculum.

# IRAN-CONTRA AFFAIR

On July 8, 1985, President Ronald Reagan told the American Bar Association that Iran was part of a "confederation of terrorist states." He failed to mention that members of his administration were secretly planning to sell weapons to Iran to facilitate the release of U.S. hostages held in Lebanon by pro-Iranian terrorist groups. Profits from the arms sales were secretly sent to Nicaragua to aid rebel forces, known as the contras, in their attempt to overthrow the country's democratically elected government. The incident became known as the Iran-Contra Affair and was the biggest scandal of Reagan's administration. The weapons sale to Iran was authorized by Robert McFarlane, head of the National Security Council (NSC), in violation of U.S. government policies regarding terrorists and military aid to Iran. NSC staff member Oliver North arranged for a portion of the $48 million paid by Iran to be sent to the contras, which violated a 1984 law banning this type of aid. North and his secretary Fawn Hall also shredded critical documents. President Reagan repeatedly denied rumors that the United States had exchanged arms for hostages, but later stated that he'd been misinformed. He created a Special Review Board to investigate. In February 1987, the board found the president not guilty. Others involved were found guilty but either had their sentences overturned on appeal or were later pardoned by George H. W. Bush.

# THE KEATING FIVE

After the banking industry was deregulated in the 1980s, savings and loan banks were allowed to invest deposits in commercial real estate, not just residential. Many savings banks began making risky investments, and the Federal Home Loan Bank Board (FHLBB) tried to stop them, against the wishes of the Reagan administration, which was against government interference with business. In 1989, when the Lincoln Savings and Loan Association of Irvine, California, collapsed, its chairman, Charles H. Keating Jr., accused the FHLBB and its former head Edwin J. Gray of conspiring against him. Gray testified that five senators had asked him to back off on the Lincoln investigation. These senators—Alan Cranston of California, Dennis DeConcini of Arizona, John Glenn of Ohio, Donald Riegle of Michigan, and John McCain of Arizona—became known as the Keating Five after it was revealed that they received a total of $1.3 million in campaign contributions from Keating. While an investigation determined that all five acted improperly, they all claimed this was a standard campaign funding practice. In August 1991, the Senate Ethics Committee recommended censure for Cranston and criticized the other four for "questionable conduct." Cranston had already decided not to run for reelection in 1992. DeConcini and Riegle served out their terms but did not run for reelection in 1994. John Glenn was reelected in 1992 and served until he retired in 1999. John McCain continues his work in the Senate.

# CHAPPAQUIDDICK SCANDAL

Since being elected to the Senate in 1962, Edward M. "Ted" Kennedy had been known as a liberal who championed causes such as education and health care, but he had less success in his personal life. On July 18, 1969, Kennedy attended a party on Chappaquiddick Island in Massachusetts. He left the party with 29-year-old Mary Jo Kopechne, who had campaigned for Ted's late brother

Robert. Soon after the two left the party, Kennedy's car veered off a bridge and Kopechne drowned. An experienced swimmer, Kennedy said he tried to rescue her but the tide was too strong. He swam to shore, went back to the party, and returned with two other men. Their rescue efforts also failed, but Kennedy waited until the next day to report the accident, calling his lawyer and Kopechne's parents first, claiming the crash had dazed him. There was speculation that he tried to cover up that he was driving under the influence, but nothing was ever proven. Kennedy pleaded guilty to leaving the scene of an accident, received a two-month suspended jail sentence, and lost his driver's license for a year. The scandal may have contributed to his failed presidential bid in 1980, but it didn't hurt his reputation in the Senate. In April 2006, *Time* magazine named him one of "America's 10 Best Senators."

# SITTING IN THE LAPS OF POWER

Former Secretary of State Henry Kissinger called power "the ultimate aphrodisiac." For centuries, influential—and married—men have been attracting women drawn by power.

## PRESIDENTIAL FOLLIES

American presidential dalliances seemed almost commonplace in the 20th century. Bill Clinton had Monica Lewinsky. Franklin D. Roosevelt had a decades-long affair with Lucy Mercer (later Rutherfurd). In fact, it was she, and not his wife Eleanor, who was with him when he died at Warm Springs, Georgia, in 1945. John Kennedy allegedly had Angie Dickinson, Marilyn Monroe, Jayne Mansfield, and Judith Campbell Exner, among others.

Warren G. Harding worked as a genial former newspaper editor and U.S. senator from Ohio before he decided to capitalize on America's war-weariness by running for president. He became the nation's 29th president in 1920, and he promised America a "return to normalcy." However, despite being married to a woman he called "Duchess," Harding had previously carried on a 15-year-long affair with Carrie Phillips, the wife of a good friend.

When that affair ended, he took up with Nan Britton, a much younger woman who was rumored to still be a virgin when she began seeing Harding. The innocence didn't last long—after one particular night of passion in the Senate Office Building in January 1919, she conceived a child. After Harding's death in 1927, Britton published a tell-all book of their trysts, *The President's Daughter*. So much for "normalcy."

## AMOROUS ALSO-RANS

Sometimes a man lusting after both the presidency and other women finds the two desires don't mix well. Such was the case in July 1791, when U.S. Treasury Secretary Alexander Hamilton began an affair with Maria Reynolds, a pretty 23-year-old woman who tearfully implored him for help as her husband had left her. A few months later Reynolds's husband James, a professional con man, mysteriously returned, and blackmailed Hamilton. Although he paid $1,750 to keep the affair quiet, Hamilton learned the sad truth that blackmailers are never satisfied. In 1797, the affair came to light, creating one of the first sex scandals in American politics. Although Hamilton apologized, many historians believe the damage to his reputation cost him the presidency he so coveted.

Another man who saw his presidential chances wrecked on

the rocks of infidelity was Gary Hart. The odds-on favorite to win the 1988 Democratic presidential nomination, the married senator from Colorado was caught by the press in April 1987, in the company of Donna Rice, a blonde 29-year-old actress and model. One of the places they had allegedly been together was on a yacht called, appropriately enough, *Monkey Business.* After several days of feverish headlines, Hart withdrew from the presidential race. Although he reentered the race later that year, Hart's monkey business had finished him as a force in national politics.

Political cost was likely not on the mind of Thomas Jefferson if, and when, he began an affair with Sally Hemings, a slave at Monticello. Although he was a powerful political figure, Jefferson was also a lonely widower who had promised his dying wife in 1782 that he would never remarry. At the time, scholars hypothesize, that he began the affair with Hemings, the presidency must have seemed a distant dream. However, in 1800, Jefferson became president. Two years later, a newspaper editor named James Callendar first published the charge that Jefferson and Hemings were an item, thus igniting a historical controversy that still rages today. Even modern methods like DNA testing have failed to positively identify Thomas Jefferson as the father of Hemings's children. The only thing certain is that this story is far from over.

## FOREIGN AFFAIRS

Of course, it is not only American political figures that have had a roving eye. Charles Stewart Parnell was a leader of the Ireland's Independence Movement in the 1880s. It seemed as if British Prime Minister William Gladstone was about to support Parnell and finally give Ireland its freedom, but in November 1890, it was revealed that Parnell had long been involved with Kitty O'Shea, the wife of William Henry O'Shea. The disclosure rocked prim-and-proper England, causing Gladstone to distance himself from Parnell and pull back from endorsing Irish independence. Thus not just a political career, but also the fate of an entire nation was affected by one man's indiscretion.

Of course, there's much more at stake than a failed political career. Claretta Pettachi was a beautiful young Italian girl who became Italian dictator Benito Mussolini's lover. To her credit (or discredit), she stayed loyal to him to the end. In April 1945, she and Mussolini were captured as they tried to flee Italy. According to legend, Pettachi was offered her freedom but refused, and she threw her body in front of Mussolini's in a vain attempt to shield him from a firing squad's bullets. Photos show their bodies, which were subsequently hung upside down in a public square.

Pettachi's devotion to her fascist lover is perhaps only topped by that of Prince Pedro of Portugal. Pedro began an affair with Inês de Castro, one of his wife's maids, who bore him two children. His wife died in 1349, and de Castro was put to death in 1355. When Pedro became king in 1357, he had his mistress's body exhumed, married the corpse, and forced his entire court to honor her remains.

History is filled with many more examples of famous men and the women they attracted. However, the attraction doesn't seem to work in the opposite direction—stories of powerful women and the men they attracted are much less common. Perhaps it is as Eleanor Roosevelt once observed: "[How] men despise women who have real power."

# 9 POLITICAL SLIPS OF THE TONGUE

Presidents and other politicians have a lot to say and not much time to say it; in their haste, the message often gets lost on its way from the brain to the mouth and comes out in funny, embarrassing, and memorable quotes. Here are some favorites.

**1** **Ronald Reagan:** As president, Reagan sometimes veered from his carefully written speeches with disastrous results. In 1988, when trying to quote John Adams, who said, "Facts are stubborn things," Reagan slipped and said, "Facts are stupid things." Not known as an environmentalist, Reagan said in 1966, "A tree is a tree. How many more do you have to look at?" His most famous blooper came during a microphone test before a 1984 radio address when he remarked, "My fellow Americans, I am pleased to tell you I just signed legislation which outlaws Russia forever. The bombing begins in five minutes."

**2** **Al Gore:** Al Gore served as vice president under Bill Clinton from 1993 to 2001. During the 1992 campaign, he asked voters skeptical of change to remember that every Communist government in Eastern Europe had fallen within 100 days, followed by, "Now it's our turn here in the United States of America." Gore has often been incorrectly quoted as saying that he invented the Internet, but his actual comment in 1999 was, "During my service in the United States Congress, I took the initiative in creating the Internet."

**3** **Richard Nixon:** Richard M. Nixon was the 37th president of the United States, serving from 1969 to 1974. He is the only U.S. president to have resigned from office. Famous for telling reporters, "I am not a crook," Nixon once gave this advice to a political associate: "You don't know how to lie. If you can't lie, you'll never go anywhere." Nixon couldn't cover up Watergate and he couldn't cover up bloopers like that either.

**4** **Richard J. Daley:** Mayor Richard J. Daley served as the undisputed leader of Chicago during the turbulent 1960s. The Democratic National Convention was held in Chicago in August 1968, but with the nation divided by the Vietnam War and the assassinations of Martin Luther King Jr. and Robert F. Kennedy fueling animosity, the city became a battleground for antiwar protests, which Americans witnessed on national television. When confrontations between protesters and police turned violent, Daley's blooper comment reflected the opinion of many people: "The police are not here to create disorder, they're here to preserve disorder."

**5** **Texas House Speaker Gib Lewis:** A true slow-talkin' Texan, many of Texas House Speaker Gib Lewis's famous bloopers may have influenced his colleague, future president George W. Bush. While closing a congressional session, Lewis's real feelings about his peers slipped out when he said, "I want to thank each and every one of you for having extinguished yourselves this session." He tried to explain his problems once by saying, "There's a lot of uncertainty that's not clear in my mind." He could have been describing his jumbled reign as Texas Speaker when he commented, "This is unparalyzed in the state's history."

**6** **Dan Quayle:** Before President George W. Bush took over the title, Dan Quayle was the reigning king of malaprops. Serving one term as vice president from 1989 to 1993, Quayle's slips of the tongue made him an easy but well-deserved target for late-night talk shows. His most famous blunder came in 1992 when, at an elementary school spelling bee in New Jersey, he corrected student William Figueroa's correct spelling of potato as p-o-t-a-t-o-e. Quayle didn't really help the campaign for reelection when, at a stop in California, he said, "This president is going to lead us out of this recovery."

**7** **Spiro Agnew:** Spiro Theodore Agnew served as vice president from 1969 to 1973 under President Nixon, before resigning following evidence of tax evasion. This slip expressed his true feelings on this matter: "I apologize for lying to you. I promise I won't deceive you except in matters of this sort." Agnew also didn't endear himself to poor people in 1968 when he commented, "To some extent, if you've seen one city slum, you've seen them all."

**8** **George W. Bush:** Reflecting about growing up in Midland, Texas, President George W. Bush said in a 1994 interview, "It was just inebriating what Midland was all about then." Back in those days, Dubya was known to be a heavy drinker, so misspeaking the word invigorating was a real Freudian slip. During his time in the White House, the junior Bush had enough malaprops to give a centipede a serious case of foot-in-the-mouth syndrome.

**9** **George H. W. Bush:** With Dan Quayle as his vice president, the bloopers of President George H. W. Bush sometimes got overshadowed, but he still managed some zingers. While campaigning in 1988, he described serving as Ronald Reagan's vice president this way, "For seven and a half years I've worked alongside President Reagan. We've had triumphs. Made some mistakes. We've had some sex... uh...setbacks." When it comes to presidents 41 and 43, you could say that the slip doesn't fall far from the tongue.

# ASSASSINATION PLOTS AGAINST FIDEL CASTRO

American intelligence agencies were very active and successful during the Cold War. But how come no one could kill the leader of Cuba?

Perhaps no human being in history survived more assassination attempts than Fidel Castro. A popular leader who overthrew the hated Cuban dictator Fulgencio Batista in 1959, Castro had first attempted to organize the people of Cuba directly into revolution, but he was thrown into prison in 1953. He had his first brush with assassination there: Batista ordered the guards to poison Castro, but none of them would do it. In 1955, after Batista made an election promise to free political prisoners, he ordered Castro's release. But the dictator was not about to let bygones be bygones. He sent an assassin named Eutimio Guerra to get close to Castro, but the revolutionary leader was suspicious of Guerra and gave him the slip. Castro seemed to lead a charmed life, and his revolutionary army moved from town to town fighting for Cuba until it was free of Batista.

After overthrowing the dictator and liberating Cuba, Castro was wildly popular with the majority of Cubans, although he was looked on with suspicion by almost everyone else. And because he received limited support from Cuba's traditional allies, including the United States, Castro had little or no choice but to ally Cuba with the Soviet Union. After all, he was just following the age-old maxim—"The enemy of my enemy is my friend." And what an enemy he made!

## BEFORE THE BAY OF PIGS

Most people think that the halfhearted backing of the Bay

of Pigs invasion was the starting gun for hostility between Castro and John F. Kennedy, but it was Dwight Eisenhower who set the "Kill Fidel Contest" in motion in 1960 with what ultimately became Operation Mongoose—400 CIA agents working full-time to remove the Cuban dictator. At first, they decided to train paramilitary guerrillas to eliminate Castro in a traditional commando operation, but his immense popularity among the Cuban people made that impossible. The CIA did all the preliminary work on the Bay of Pigs. Then Eisenhower left office, and Kennedy came upon the scene.

The Bay of Pigs invasion turned out to be a fiasco, and a year and a half later the Cuban Missile Crisis almost triggered a full-scale nuclear war. America's only answer seemed to be to get rid of Fidel and try to turn Cuba back into a pliant banana republic (or in this case, sugarcane republic). But who would do it—and how?

## WHO'S UP TO THE JOB?

The problem was that everyone wanted to get in on the act. The U.S. government hated having a Soviet base 90 miles from Florida. Batista Cubans, who'd lost their big-moneyed businesses, wanted their privileged lives back. Anti-communists such as FBI boss J. Edgar Hoover viewed a plot to assassinate Castro as a struggle against elemental evil. American businesses that relied on sugar felt the loss of their cheap supply. The Mafia, which had owned lucrative casinos and brothels in Havana, wanted revenge. As it turned out, the Mafia had the best shot—and they had help.

The CIA, not being able to handle the job themselves, hired Mafia members to terminate Castro with extreme prejudice. In exchange, the CIA pressured the FBI to offer the Mafia a certain amount of immunity in the United States. But the

Mafia got used to the new leniency, which would end if Castro were killed, so they strung the agency along with false promises to kill Castro if the CIA would continue to protect them from the FBI. Meanwhile, President Kennedy grew impatient. Changing the name of Operation Mongoose to Operation Freedom, he sent the American intelligence community in a full-time rush to whack Fidel. But after the Bay of Pigs, intelligence planners believed that conventional measures wouldn't work, so the attempts became stranger:

• During a United Nations meeting at which Castro was present, an agent working for the CIA managed to slip a poisoned cigar into Fidel's cigar case, but someone figured it out before Castro could light up.

• Another idea was to send Castro on an acid trip by dosing his cigars with LSD. He would appear psychotic, and his sanity would be questioned. When this story finally came out, it merely gave a lot of old hippies a few laughs.

• Castro was an avid scuba diver, so the CIA sprayed the inside of a wet suit with tuberculosis germs and a fungal skin disease called Madura foot. Then they gave it to a lawyer heading to Havana to negotiate the release of Bay of Pigs prisoners. He was supposed to give the suit to Castro, but at the last minute the lawyer decided that the plot was too obvious and was an embarrassment to the United States, so he didn't take the suit with him.

• Perhaps the most famous dumb idea of all was to find out where Fidel's favorite diving spot was and prepare an exploding conch shell to kill him, but for many obvious reasons this plan was dropped as being unfeasible.

• Traditional assassination methods were also tried. Cuban exiles were sent to Havana with high-powered rifles and telescopic sights to take care of the problem with good old-fashioned lead, but none of them could get close enough to shoot Castro.

• One of Castro's guards was given a poison pen that worked like a hypodermic needle, but he was discovered before he could get close enough to inject the leader.

Starting in the 1970s, the CIA seemed to lose interest in these plans, and thereafter most attempts to kill the leader were carried out by Cuban exiles (with CIA funding, of course), who had made hating Castro almost a religion. Fabian Escalante, Castro's head of security, claimed that there had been 638 plots to kill Castro.

Fidel Castro died of natural causes on November 25, 2016, at age 90.

# CLEVELAND'S SECRET CANCER

Grover Cleveland, the only man elected president of the United States to two nonconsecutive terms, was known as "Grover the Good" for his honesty. However, there was one time when Cleveland was not very honest.

## THE PAINFUL TRUTH

In 1893, Cleveland had only recently returned to the White House, this time as the 24th president. America had just entered a national economic depression, the Panic of 1893. To help the economy recover, Cleveland wanted to repeal the Sherman Silver Purchase Act and maintain the gold standard.

On June 13, 1893, Cleveland had some pain on the left—or the "cigar-chewing"—side of the roof of his mouth. A few days later, he noticed a rough spot in the area as well. Five days later, he asked White House physician R. M. O'Reilly to take a look. The doctor discovered a cauliflower-like area the size of a quarter in the president's mouth. Samples were sent to several doctors for biopsy, and the results came back as malignant. Cleveland's close friend Dr. Joseph Bryant reportedly said to him, "Were it in my mouth, I would have it removed at once."

## WE'VE GOT A SECRET

But having surgery wasn't that easy. With the economy on the skids, the country jittery, and a pro-silver vice president (Adlai Stevenson), Cleveland did not want to further upset the nation by announcing that his health was at risk. So he ordered his condition be kept secret from the public.

But his medical team was racing against a deadline. It was now late June. Congress would reconvene on August 7, and Cleveland wanted to have recovered enough to personally campaign to persuade wavering congressmen to vote for free silver repeal. Meanwhile, the doctors were desperate to perform the surgery and stop the cancer from spreading.

It was agreed the surgery was to be conducted on July 1. For maximum secrecy, the operation was to be held on the yacht *Oneida*, owned by the president's friend Commodore Elias Benedict. This was logical; Cleveland was often seen on Benedict's yacht, and with the July 4th holiday approaching it was an entirely plausible place for him to be.

## SINK OR SWIM

The doctors had already slipped on board when Cleveland joined them on June 30. The yacht was floating in Bellevue Bay in New York City's East River—near Bellevue Hospital. Around noon on July 1, Cleveland went below deck and was propped up in a chair that was lashed to the mast. Fifty-six years old and corpulent, Cleveland was considered at high risk for a stroke if ether was used as an anesthetic. Dr. Bryant decided to use nitrous oxide instead and hope for the best. Bryant was so anxious about the operation and Cleveland's condition that he told the captain that if he hit a rock he should really hit it, so that they would all go to the bottom.

Over the next few hours, doctors removed Cleveland's entire left upper jaw, from the first bicuspid to past the last molar. Cleveland recovered in splendid isolation aboard the yacht for a few days, and then for a few weeks at his family's Cape Cod vacation home. A plug of vulcanized rubber was made to fill the huge hole in Cleveland's jaw. The press was told that Cleveland had been treated aboard the ship for two ulcerated teeth and rheumatism and was recovering nicely. (Oh, and by the way, the free silver repeal did indeed pass Congress later that year, just as Cleveland had planned.)

## NIXON WOULD HAVE BEEN PROUD

That's where matters stayed for two decades. Even though a gabby doctor spilled the beans to the *Philadelphia Press* in late August 1898, in a wonderful pre-Watergate stonewalling effort, Cleveland's doctors and close friends managed to deny the story out of existence. Finally, in 1917—nine years after Cleveland's death—the full story was finally revealed in the *Saturday Evening Post*. Today, part of Cleveland's jaw can be seen at the Mütter Museum in Philadelphia.

# WILBUR MILLS

During the Great Depression, Wilbur Mills served as a county judge in Arkansas and initiated government-funded programs to pay medical and prescription drug bills for the poor. Mills was elected to the House of Representatives in 1939 and served until 1977, with 18 of those years as head of the Ways and Means Committee. In the 1960s, Mills played an integral role in the creation of the Medicare program, and he made an unsuccessful bid for president in the 1972 primary. Unfortunately for Mills, he's best known for one of Washington's juiciest scandals. On October 7, 1974, Mills's car was stopped by police in West Potomac Park near the Jefferson Memorial. Mills was drunk and in the back seat of the car with an Argentine stripper named Fanne Foxe. When the police approached, Foxe fled the car. Mills checked into an alcohol treatment center and was reelected to Congress in November 1974. But just one month later, Mills was seen drunk onstage with Fanne Foxe. Following the incident, Mills was forced to resign as chairman of the Ways and Means Committee and did not run for reelection in 1976. Mills died in 1992, and despite the scandal, several schools and highways in Arkansas are named for him.

# TEXAS POLITICAL SCANDALS

Next to football, politics may be the most popular sport in Texas. But with politics often comes scandal, and Texas has had more than its fill of that.

• **Johnson wins by a nose:** Controversy dogged Lyndon Johnson in his first two runs for the U.S. Senate. In 1941, the member of Congress and future president ran for a vacant Senate seat in a special election against Texas governor W. Lee "Pappy" O'Daniel. Johnson initially appeared to be the winner but lost when some questionable returns were counted. He ran again in 1948, finishing second in a three-way Democratic primary to Coke Stevenson, but a runoff was forced when Stevenson failed to win a majority. Johnson won the runoff by 87 votes amidst accusations of fraud, including one that involved votes brought in by campaign manager (and future governor) John B. Connally that appeared to have been cast in alphabetical order. After a friendly judge struck down Stevenson's appeal, Johnson went on to win the general election.

- **Estes donates soiled money:** Billy Sol Estes was both a friend and an enemy of Lyndon Johnson. As a wealthy fertilizer salesman, Estes contributed to Johnson's campaigns for the Senate and the vice presidency. Unbeknownst to Johnson, much of Estes's wealth came from sources as odorous as his fertilizer. In the late 1950s, Estes lied about buying cotton from local farmers to obtain bank loans for nonexistent cotton and fertilizer he claimed was in storage. After his accountant and a government investigator died under suspicious circumstances, Estes and three associates were indicted on 57 counts of fraud. Two of these indicted associates also died suspiciously. Estes was found guilty of fraud and sentenced to eight years in prison, with an additional 15 years tacked on for other charges. His association with Johnson nearly caused President Kennedy to dump his vice president. The U.S. Supreme Court ultimately overturned Estes's conviction in 1965, however, on the grounds that having TV cameras and reporters in the courtroom (uncommon at that time) deprived him of a fair trial. After Johnson's death, Estes accused his one-time friend of involvement in a conspiracy behind the Kennedy assassination.

• **Bribery makes real estate deals easier:** The Texas Sharpstown Scandal is named for the Sharpstown master-planned community near Houston and its backer, banker and insurance company manager Frank Sharp. Sharp made loans of $600,000 from his bank to state officials, who then bought stock in his insurance company. They next passed legislation to inflate the value of the insurance company, which allowed the officials to sell their stock profitably. The huge profits aroused the suspicions of the Securities and Exchange Commission in 1971, and charges were filed against Sharp and others. The governor, lieutenant governor, and House speaker, among other state officials, were accused of bribery. Sharp received three years' probation and a $5,000 fine. One victim of the fraud, Strake Jesuit College Preparatory, lost $6 million.

• **Questionable congressional ethics:** Democrat Jim Wright represented Texas in Congress for 34 years, serving as Speaker of the House from 1987 to '89. In 1988, Republican Newt Gingrich led an investigation by the House Ethics Committee into charges that Wright used bulk purchases of his book to get around congressional limits on speaking fees and that his wife had been given a job to get around a limit on political gifts. Wright was forced to resign from Congress in 1989, and Gingrich eventually became Speaker of the House with his own subsequent ethics violations.

• **Corruption as a lifestyle:** George Parr was a political force in Duval County from the 1920s to the '60s. Replacing his brother in 1926 as county judge, Parr used legal and illegal tactics to convince the county's majority Mexican American population to support the Democratic Party. Parr was convicted of income tax evasion in 1934 and served nine months with little effect on his influence as the "Duke of

Duval County." He found questionable votes to help Lyndon Johnson win the 1948 Democratic senatorial primary and was linked to but never accused of at least three murders of political opponents. While appealing a conviction and five-year sentence for federal income tax evasion in 1975, Parr committed suicide.

# WARREN G. HARDING

Few presidents have had a reputation such as that of Warren G. Harding, the publisher-turned-politician who, after a landslide presidential victory, wrought havoc upon the United States for two years before dying while in office.

A businessman, Freemason, and consummate Republican, Warren G. Harding was born not far from Marion, Ohio, in 1865. He remained there for much of his adult life, becoming a prominent member of the business community before entering political life in 1898. He served two terms as a state senator and briefly held the post of lieutenant governor before running an unsuccessful gubernatorial campaign. But after introducing fellow Ohioan and then-nominee for the presidency William Howard Taft at the 1912 Republican National Convention, Harding, who was by all accounts a captivating but hollow orator, quickly rose to political stardom.

He was elected to the U.S. Senate two years later and by 1920 was campaigning for the White House. Harding became the Republican candidate for president only as the result of a deadlock between the other candidates, but he nevertheless defeated James M. Cox, the Democratic governor of Harding's native Ohio, in a landslide victory with a little more than 60 percent of the popular vote.

## THE OHIO GANG

Harding's presidency is not usually revered for its policy, which sought to overturn major legislation from the Wilson administration, deregulate large businesses, and limit American involvement in international affairs. Most historians agree that Harding's policies contributed greatly to the economic collapse at the end of the 1920s. Still, Harding performed the ceremonial functions that officially brought World War I to a close, supported both the railroads and domestic agriculture, and created the federal budget. Though he died in the middle of his first term, many of his policy goals were carried out by his successors: Calvin Coolidge, his vice president, and Herbert Hoover, his secretary of commerce.

However destructive they may have been, Harding's failed policies have been largely overshadowed by the magnitude of his administration's corruption, which included fraud, bribery, embezzlement, and drug and alcohol trafficking. The most serious offense was the Teapot Dome scandal, when Secretary of the Interior Albert B. Hall illegally leased government land (the Teapot Dome oil field in Wyoming) to oil companies in exchange for bribes and under-the-table private loans. Hall and other members of the administration—known as the Ohio Gang, though none actually hailed from the Buckeye State—were forced to resign amidst a sea of public outrage; Hall went to prison, and his colleague Jess Smith committed suicide.

## AND THAT'S NOT ALL

Though the Teapot Dome affair went on under Harding's watch, many historians question whether he was even aware of the corruption in his cabinet. The only offense attributed directly to Harding is his rumored alcoholism. Despite his unwavering support for Prohibition, Harding was, by all accounts, a drunkard, regularly consuming contraband liquor in the White House even when it was against federal law to do so. For good measure, he was also accused of fathering a child out of wedlock with a fawning admirer from Marion named Nan Britton. Britton made the accusations public when she published a lurid account of their supposed relationship, *The President's Daughter*, in 1927.

Harding died of a heart attack in 1923 after less than two and a half years in office. He is regularly ranked among the worst presidents in U.S. history, both for the rampant corruption in his administration and his support of policies that discouraged regulation and indirectly led to the Great Depression. Perhaps that's why no Ohioan has been elected president since.

# EDWARD HYDE: CROSS-DRESSER OR DOUBLE-CROSSED?

Edward Hyde, Viscount Cornbury, Third Earl of Clarendon, was governor of New York and New Jersey from 1701 to 1708, yet his legacy is one that politicians wouldn't want to touch with a ten-foot pole. Aside from doing a generally terrible job, rumors of Hyde's cross-dressing ways landed him a sullied spot in the annals of political history.

## HERE, HAVE A JOB!

As the story goes, being of noble English lineage, Edward Hyde was able to buy an officer's commission in the British army. While in that position, he helped overthrow his commander (and uncle), King James II. The king who replaced James was William III, who was quite pleased with

Hyde's assistance in getting him the throne, so in 1701, William made Hyde governor of New York as a way of saying thanks. Later, William's successor (and Hyde's first cousin), Queen Anne, also threw in the governorship of New Jersey for Hyde. Suddenly, a woefully under-qualified guy from England was in charge of two of the most prominent colonies in the New World.

## CORRUPTION, COLONIAL STYLE

When Hyde arrived in New York in 1703 to assume his new post, he didn't make a very good impression with the struggling, toiling colonists. His luxurious house was filled with sumptuous linens, curtains, silverware, furniture, and art. To make matters worse, he soon found it necessary to divert public defense funds toward his new country house on what was then christened "Governor's Island."

It didn't take long for the bribery to start. At first, Hyde reportedly turned down a bribe from a New Jersey proprietor, but it appears he only passed because the bribe wasn't big enough. The man, hoping to get preferential treatment of some kind, then upped the ante. Hyde accepted the bribe the second time around and did the businessman's bidding. Soon, a group of the governor's favorites controlled tax and rent collections across the area. The bribes were constant, and the governor sank deeper and deeper into corruption. He was described at one point as "a spendthrift, a grafter, a bigoted oppressor and a drunken vain fool."

By 1707, a desperate New Jersey assembly wrote to Queen Anne to take Hyde back to Britain. One assembly member, Lewis Morris, made a list of Hyde's crimes and added a juicy bit: He claimed the corrupt governor was fond of dressing in women's clothing. That item of gossip didn't sit well with the queen, and Hyde lost his job. What isn't often mentioned is that Hyde, thrown into disgrace (and into debtor's prison) for some time, actually rallied later in life and held office in England where he was a respected diplomat of the Privy Council.

## RIGHT THIS WAY, MRS. HYDE?

The question remains whether Hyde really was a cross-dresser or just the victim of a rumor drummed up by his enemies to help push him out of office. One story tells of Hyde costumed as Queen Anne in order to show deference and respect—but could that really be true?

According to certain historians, there is no hard evidence that Hyde was fond of wearing dresses. Only four contemporary letters contain any information pertaining to his cross-dressing, and they don't include eyewitness accounts. Experts maintain that if the governor of New York and New Jersey really did don full petticoats and silk taffeta, it would have been plastered across every newspaper in the Western Hemisphere—people in the 18th century loved a scandal as much as people do now.

Still, the rumors persisted for years and stories of his behavior grew—there is even a period portrait of a scruffy man in women's clothing that is said to be Hyde. Yet, art historians say there's no proof that the painting is of anyone other than an unfortunate-looking young woman.

# ELIOT SPITZER'S SEXUAL SHENANIGANS

Eliot Spitzer was the governor of New York and a promising up-and-comer in the Democratic Party until 2008, when he was fingered in a federal investigation that publicly revealed his penchant for high-priced call girls.

The revelation had a devastating effect on Spitzer's political career, which had been built on his reputation as a squeaky-clean foe of organized crime and political corruption. The fact that the governor had been cheating on his wife was bad enough, political analysts noted, but more damning was the obvious fact that he was a bald-faced hypocrite.

Caught red-handed, Spitzer may have felt he had no choice but to resign as governor. After more than a year of lying low, he reentered the public eye as a political commentator. Observers' opinions are mixed as to whether he might one day seek political office again.

# A GAY TIME IN THE OVAL OFFICE?

Before he became U.S. president, the unmarried James Buchanan enjoyed a long, close association with his housemate, William R. King—so close that unconfirmed speculation about the pair still swirls after more than 150 years. Was Buchanan—the nation's only bachelor chief executive—also its first homosexual president?

The year 1834 was a momentous one for 42-year-old James Buchanan. Already a veteran political leader and diplomat, Buchanan won a seat in the U.S. Senate and formed a friendship with the man who would be his dearest companion for the next two decades.

Buchanan and his chum, William Rufus de Vane King, a U.S. senator from Alabama, became virtually inseparable. They shared quarters in Washington, D.C., for 15 years. Capitol wits referred to the partners—who attended social events together—as "the Siamese twins."

Buchanan's bond with Senator King was so close that the future president described it as a "communion." In praising his friend as "among the best, purest, and most consistent public men I have ever known," Buchanan added that King was a "very gay, elegant-looking fellow." The adjective "gay," however, didn't mean "homosexual" back then. It commonly meant "merry."

It's also useful to understand that it was not unusual for educated men to wax rhapsodic about other men during the 19th century. Admiring rather than sexual, this sort of language signified shared values and deep respect.

Historians rightly point out a lack of evidence that either of the bachelors found men sexually attractive. They note that when Buchanan was younger, he asked a Pennsylvania heiress to marry him. (She broke off the engagement.) Later, he was known to flirt with fashionable women.

## BUCHANAN'S "WIFE"

Whatever the nature of his relationship with Buchanan, King seemed to consider it something more than casual. After the Alabaman became U.S. minister to France in 1844, he wrote home from Paris, expressing his worry that Buchanan would "procure an associate who will cause you to feel no regret at our separation."

Buchanan did not find such a replacement, but it was apparently not for want of trying. He wrote to another friend of his attempts to ease the loneliness caused by King's absence: "I have gone a wooing to several gentlemen, but have not succeeded with any one of them...."

Sometimes the pair drew derisive jibes from their peers. The jokes often targeted King, a bit of a dandy with a fondness for silk scarves. In a private letter, Tennessee Congressman

Aaron V. Brown used the pronoun "she" to refer to the senator, and called him Buchanan's "wife." President Andrew Jackson mocked King as "Miss Nancy" and "Aunt Fancy."

## HIGH-FLYING CAREERS DERAILED

Despite the childish jokes, both Buchanan and King advanced to ever-more-important federal posts. President James K. Polk selected Buchanan as his secretary of state in 1845. King won the office of U.S. vice president (running on a ticket with Franklin Pierce) in 1852. Voters elected Buchanan to the White House four years later.

Unfortunately, neither of the friends distinguished himself in the highest office he reached. King fell ill and died less than a month after taking the oath as vice president.

Erupting conflicts over slavery and states' rights marred Buchanan's single term in the Oval Office. Historians give him failing marks for his lack of leadership as the Civil War loomed. The pro-slavery chief executive (he was a Pennsylvania Democrat) opposed secession of the Southern states but argued that the federal government had no authority to use force to stop it. As a result, Buchanan made no effort to save the Union, leaving that task to his successor, Abraham Lincoln.

## WHAT'S SEX GOT TO DO WITH IT?

Would Buchanan have risen to the highest office in the land if his peers honestly believed he was homosexual? It's hard to say. Today's perception is that 19th-century Americans were more homophobic than their 21st-century descendants. Yet in an era when sexuality stayed tucked beneath Victorian wraps, there was a de facto "don't ask, don't tell" policy for virtually any profession. Whatever their private proclivities, Buchanan and King clearly excelled in their public lives—at least until Buchanan got into the White House. Based on what little evidence history provides, neither man's sexual orientation had much, if any, bearing on what he accomplished, or failed to accomplish, in his career.

# ALEXANDER HAMILTON: SUICIDE BY DUEL?

The duel between Aaron Burr and Alexander Hamilton in Weehawken, New Jersey, is one of the most discussed events in American history. Yet many questions remain unanswered about the affair. Did Hamilton go to the duel determined to die?

The tension and the anger had been building for years. Accusations and insults were flung back and forth between former Secretary of the Treasury Alexander Hamilton and U.S. Vice President Aaron Burr. After Burr's stint with President Thomas Jefferson was finished, he ran for governor of New York in 1804. Hamilton did everything he could to undermine Burr's credibility in the race, and Burr was subsequently defeated. In April, the *Albany Register* published a (originally private) letter, in which it was reported that Hamilton had said some nasty things about Burr. Burr demanded an apology, but Hamilton danced around the matter.

Furious, Burr ultimately challenged Hamilton to a duel on July 11, 1804, which ended Hamilton's life and Burr's political career. Hurt feelings and honor aside, many historians consider the reasons for the duel flimsy at best and have debated for years over Hamilton's exact intentions for participating in it.

## WASTED SHOT

Some historians feel that Hamilton was depressed and suicidal, and that he goaded Burr so as to force the duel to occur. As writer and historian Henry Adams wrote, "Instead of killing Burr, [Hamilton] invited Burr to kill him." In Ron Chernow's 2004 biography of Hamilton, he cites four psycho-biographers who in 1978 concluded that the duel was a disguised form of suicide by Hamilton.

The reasons given for Hamilton's depression are several: His son Philip was killed in a duel in 1801; he realized that there was no place for him in national politics now that his rival Thomas Jefferson was president; and he had severely weakened the Federalist political party, which he helped create, by attacking its candidate for president (John Adams) in 1800.

In the book *A Fatal Friendship: Alexander Hamilton and Aaron Burr*, author Arnold Rogow maintains that Hamilton was a manic depressive who was severely depressed over his own physical maladies and the death of George Washington in 1799, and that his deteriorating condition led him to push for the duel.

A reason often cited by "pro-suicidal" historians as proof of Hamilton's queasy mental state is that he decided before the duel to "throw away his fire," or waste his first shot. This is seen by many as an invitation by Hamilton to be killed by Burr.

## A GAMBLE LOST

However, others say the duel was inevitable. They point out that although Hamilton was morally against dueling, he was also bound by 19th century codes of honor. He could not back out once Burr had challenged him. After all, he did attack Burr's character.

In a letter to his wife written the night before, Hamilton says that he did not want to fight: "If it had been possible for me to have avoided the interview, my love for you and my precious children would have been alone a decisive motive."

Chernow postulates that Hamilton gambled that Burr would not shoot to kill. Dueling was outlawed in the northern states, and both men knew that Burr would be labeled a murderer and politically destroyed if he killed Hamilton. In another letter written the night before his impending duel, Hamilton said, "I have resolved, if our interview is conducted in the usual manner, and it pleases God to give me the opportunity, to reserve and throw away my first fire, and I have thoughts even of reserving my second fire."

Perhaps Hamilton viewed the duel as nothing more than a dare and counter-dare. He had, after all, taken part in ten previous shotless duels.

Whether Hamilton went into the duel meaning to die or not, his death remains a cold hard fact. Burr's shot hit Hamilton in the abdomen, damaging his ribs and several internal organs. When Burr later heard of what Hamilton had written about wasting his shot, he reportedly responded, "Contemptible, if true."

# STEALING THE PRESIDENT

While he was alive, President Abraham Lincoln was loved and admired by many. Perhaps his popularity was the reason why in 1876, a group of men decided that people would be willing to pay a lot of money to see the 16th president of the United States—even if he was dead.

## BREAKING OUT BOYD

The plot was hatched in 1876, 11 years after President Lincoln's assassination by John Wilkes Booth. Illinois engraver Benjamin Boyd had been arrested on charges of creating engraving plates to make counterfeit bills. Boyd's boss, James "Big Jim" Kinealy, a man known around Chicago as the King of the Counterfeiters, was determined to get Boyd out of prison in order to continue his counterfeiting operation.

Kinealy's plan was to kidnap Lincoln's corpse from his mausoleum at the Oak Ridge Cemetery in Springfield, Illinois, and hold it for ransom—$200,000 in cash and a full pardon for Boyd. Not wanting to do the dirty work himself, Kinealy turned to two men: John "Jack" Hughes and Terrence Mullen, a bartender at The Hub, a Madison Street bar frequented by Kinealy and his associates.

Kinealy told Hughes and Mullen that they were to steal Lincoln's body on Election Night, November 7, load it onto a cart, and take it roughly 200 miles north to the shores of Lake Michigan. They were to bury the body in the sand, stowing it until the ransom was paid. The plan seemed foolproof until Hughes and Mullen decided they needed a third person to help steal the body—a fellow named Lewis Swegles. It was a decision Hughes and Mullen would come to regret.

## THE PLAN BACKFIRES

The man directly responsible for bringing Boyd in was Patrick D. Tyrrell, a member of the Secret Service in Chicago. Long before their current role of protecting the president of the United States, one of the main jobs for members of the Secret Service was to track down and arrest counterfeiters. One of Tyrrell's informants was a small-time crook by the name of Lewis Swegles. Yes, the same guy who agreed to help Hughes and Mullen steal the president's body. Thanks to the stool pigeon, everything the duo was planning was being reported back to the Secret Service.

On the evening of November 7, 1876, Hughes, Mullen, and Swegles entered the Lincoln Mausoleum, unaware of the Secret Service lying in wait. The hoods broke open Lincoln's sarcophagus and removed the casket, and Swegles was sent to get the wagon. Swegles gave the signal to make the arrest, but once the Secret Service men reached the mausoleum, they found it to be empty. In all the confusion, Hughes and Mullen had slipped away, leaving Lincoln's body behind.

Unsure what to do next, Tyrrell ordered Swegles back to Chicago to see if he could pick up the kidnappers' trail. Swegles eventually found them in a local Chicago tavern, and on November 16 or 17 (sources vary), Hughes and Mullen were arrested without incident.

## LINCOLN IS LAID TO REST (AGAIN)

With no laws on the books at the time pertaining to the stealing of a body, Hughes and Mullen were only charged with attempted larceny of Lincoln's coffin and a count each of conspiracy. After a brief trial, both men were found guilty. Their sentence for attempting to steal the body of President Abraham Lincoln: One year in the Illinois state penitentiary in Joliet.

As for Lincoln's coffin, it remains at its home in Oak Ridge Cemetery; it has been moved an estimated 17 times and opened 6 times. On September 26, 1901, the Lincoln family took steps to ensure Abe's body could never be stolen again: It was buried 10 feet under the floor of the mausoleum, inside a metal cage, and under thousands of pounds of concrete.

# BILLY GRAHAM'S MOMENTS OF CONTROVERSY

Many evangelists have become internationally renowned through their efforts to spread God's word, but few have achieved the level of international acclaim experienced by Billy Graham. Over the years, his astoundingly popular evangelical crusades filled stadiums—and instilled the Holy Spirit in the hearts of millions.

Graham was very cognizant of the image of evangelists as con men who preyed on the poor, and he vowed early on to live a life free of scandal and without a hint of opportunism. He made sure that the finances of his ministry were transparent, and as a result he managed to avoid the travails that afflicted many of his contemporaries. In fact, the Billy Graham Evangelistic Association's annual reports are available online at their website for everyone to review.

As a result of his pristine image, Graham was sought out by many of the world's most influential leaders. Over the course of his career, he met and prayed with every president from Harry Truman to Barack Obama. President George W. Bush told Graham that it was a conversation with him that led Bush to become a born-again Christian.

Always eager to save one more soul, Graham reached out to Christians every way he could: through television, several best-selling books, a newspaper advice column, and even motion pictures such as *Two a Penny* (1967), in which he played himself.

## CONTROVERSIAL MOMENTS

Graham's life was not perfect, however, and over the years there were some controversial moments. In the 1950s, he endorsed Senator Joseph McCarthy in what would later become known as McCarthy's communist "witch hunt," and in 2002 Graham was embarrassed by the release of a taped conversation with President Richard Nixon in which Graham said, "...a lot of the Jews are great friends of mine, they swarm around me and are friendly to me because they know that I'm friendly with Israel. But they don't know how I really feel about what they are doing to this country." Graham has also been criticized for not doing more to address the nation's social ills, such as civil rights, and for being too close to men of power.

# INDECENT PROPOSAL

Did President Grover Cleveland really claim a 9-year-old girl as his future wife? Reader, he married her.

President Cleveland was one of very few bachelors to be elected U.S. president. In the 1870s, already almost middle aged, he was asked about his continued bachelorhood. He called dibs on the young girl who would eventually become his wife, although at the time she was just 9.

He was reported to say: "I'm only waiting for my wife to grow up."

True to his word, he wed Frances Folsom in the Blue Room of the White House on June 2, 1886, an event that turned

Folsom into the youngest first lady in our nation's history: Cleveland was 49 years old, and Folsom was just 21.

# LINCOLN ASSASSINATION THEORIES

On April 14, 1865, President Abraham Lincoln was shot in the head by stage actor John Wilkes Booth while attending the play *Our American Cousin* at Ford's Theatre in Washington, D.C. President Lincoln died the following morning. Questions and conspiracy theories about who may or may not have been involved with Booth arose almost immediately and continue to be debated today.

## SIMPLE CONSPIRACY LED BY BOOTH

Most historians agree that Lincoln's assassination was the culmination of a plot by John Wilkes Booth and several other conspirators to kill Lincoln, Vice President Andrew Johnson, and Secretary of State William H. Seward. According to this theory, the entire plot consisted simply of John Wilkes Booth as the leader of a small group of coconspirators attempting to save the Confederate cause. Initially, Booth planned to kidnap Lincoln and then ransom him for captive Confederate soldiers, but the conspiracy evolved into the first presidential assassination in U.S. history.

Conspirators Samuel Arnold, George Atzerodt, David Herold, Lewis Powell, John Surratt, and Michael O'Laughlen all joined with Booth to design various plots that would achieve victory for the South and cause trouble for Lincoln and his backers. Arnold, John Surratt, and O'Laughlen later swore that they knew nothing of the plot to commit murder, but Atzerodt, Herold, and Powell most certainly did. They each had their own assigned roles in the grand assassination plot, unsuccessful though they were in carrying out those parts. Atzerodt was slated to assassinate Vice President Andrew Johnson, while Powell and Herold were scheduled to kill Secretary of State William Seward. All three assassinations were planned for the same time on the evening of April 14. Only Booth found complete success in the mission, however.

## CONSPIRACY INVOLVING SECRETARY OF WAR EDWIN STANTON

One of the most lasting conspiracy theories was put forth in Otto Eisenschiml's 1937 book *Why Was Lincoln Murdered*. The book claims that Lincoln's Secretary of War, Edwin Stanton, was directly involved in the assassination. Eisenschiml argued that Stanton was against Lincoln's lenient Reconstruction policies and wanted him out of the way so that a more radical Reconstructionist policy could be employed.

On the day of the assassination, General Ulysses S. Grant was expected to attend the play with the Lincolns, but Eisenschiml claimed that Stanton ordered Grant to cancel. Eisenschiml argued that had Grant attended, the military guards who protected him would never have allowed Booth to enter the president's theater box. Stanton also allegedly refused the president's request to have Major Thomas T. Eckert serve as his bodyguard for the evening, falsely stating that Eckert had critical work to do at the War Department's Telegraph Office.

After Lincoln was shot, Stanton allegedly failed to alert the security at the Navy Yard Bridge, over which Booth escaped. Eisenschiml also alleged that Stanton secretly arranged for Booth to be killed rather than arrested and suppressed evidence by removing pages from Booth's diary.

## CONSPIRACY INVOLVING VICE PRESIDENT ANDREW JOHNSON

Some conspiracy theorists suggest that Vice President Andrew Johnson was involved in the assassination plot. On the afternoon before shooting the president, Booth paid a visit to the hotel where Johnson was staying. Finding the vice president wasn't there, Booth left a note, "Don't wish to disturb you; are you at home?" Lincoln's wife, Mary Todd Lincoln, wrote in a letter to her friend that she thought Johnson was involved. Some members of Congress also thought Johnson was involved and set up a special committee to investigate Johnson's role. The committee ultimately failed to find sufficient evidence linking Johnson to Lincoln's death.

# WHO SHOT JFK?

Perhaps no conspiracy theories are more popular than the ones involving that afternoon in Dallas—November 22, 1963—when the United States lost a president. John F. Kennedy's life and death have reached out to encompass everyone from Marilyn Monroe to Fidel Castro, Sam Giancana to J. Edgar Hoover.

- **Single-shooter theory:** This is the one the Warren Commission settled on—that Lee Harvey Oswald (and only Lee Harvey Oswald), firing his Mannlicher-Carcano rifle from the window of the Texas Book Depository, killed the president in Dealey Plaza. This is the official finding.

- **Two-shooter theory:** A second shooter on the nearby grassy knoll fired at the same time as Oswald. His bullets hit Texas Governor John Connally and struck President Kennedy from the front. This theory arose after U.S. Marine sharpshooters at Quantico tried to duplicate the single-shooter theory but found it was impossible for all the shots to have come from the Book Depository.

- **LBJ theory:** Lyndon Johnson's mistress, Madeleine Brown, said that the vice president met with powerful Texans the night before the killing. She claimed he told her, "After tomorrow those goddamn Kennedys will never embarrass me again—that's no threat—that's a promise." Jack Ruby also implicated LBJ, as did E. Howard Hunt, just before his death.

- **CIA theory:** After Kennedy forced Allen Dulles to resign as head of the CIA following the Bay of Pigs fiasco, the CIA, resenting Kennedy's interference, took its revenge on the president. They'd had plenty of practice helping plotters take out Patrice Lumumba of the Congo, Rafael Trujillo of the Dominican Republic, and President Ngo Dinh Diem of Vietnam.

- **Cuban exiles theory:** Reflecting more bitterness over the Bay of Pigs, the powerful Cuban exile community in the United States was eager to see Kennedy dead and said so. However, this probably played no part in the assassination.

- **J. Edgar Hoover and the Mafia theory:** The Mafia was said to have been blackmailing Hoover about his homosexuality for ages. The theory goes that when Attorney General Robert F. Kennedy began to legally pursue Jimmy Hoffa and Mafia bosses in Chicago, Tampa, and New Orleans, they sent Hoover after JFK as payback.

• **Organized crime theory:** Chicago Mafia boss Sam Giancana, who supposedly shared the affections of Marilyn Monroe with both JFK and RFK—using Frank Sinatra as a go-between—felt betrayed when RFK went after the mob. After all, hadn't they fixed JFK's 1960 election?

• **Soviet theory:** High-ranking Soviet defector Ion Pacepa said that Soviet intelligence chiefs believed that the KGB had orchestrated the Dallas killing. But they were probably just bragging.

• **Roscoe White theory:** According to White's son, this Dallas police officer was part of a three-man assassination team. The junior White, however, gives no indication of the reasons behind the plot.

• **Saul theory:** A professional hit man was paid $50,000 to kill Kennedy by a group of very powerful, unknown men. He was also supposed to kill Oswald. Clearly, this theory isn't thick with details.

• **Castro theory:** Supposedly the Cuban government contracted Oswald to kill Kennedy, telling him that there was an escape plan. There wasn't.

• **Israeli theory:** Angry with JFK for pressuring them not to develop nuclear weapons and/or for employing ex-Nazis in the space program, the Israelis supposedly conspired in his assassination.

• **Federal Reserve theory:** Kennedy issued Executive Order 11110, enabling the U.S. Treasury to print silver certificates in an attempt to drain the silver reserves. It is theorized that such a development would severely limit the economic power of the Federal Reserve. Could this have played into his assassination?

# MLK ASSASSINATION THEORIES

On the evening of April 4, 1968, civil rights leader Reverend Martin Luther King Jr. was standing on a second-floor balcony at the Lorraine Motel in Memphis, Tennessee, where he was to lead a protest march on behalf of striking garbage workers, when he was felled by an assassin's bullet.

Shortly after the shot was fired, witnesses saw a man believed to be James Earl Ray fleeing from the scene of the assassination, and a rifle found near the site had Ray's fingerprints on it. James Earl Ray pleaded guilty to King's murder in 1969 and was sentenced to 99 years in prison, though he later recanted his confession and spent the rest of his life claiming King's death was part of a conspiracy. Dr. King's widow later said she believed Ray either did not act alone or had no role at all.

The United States House of Representatives Select Committee on Assassinations (HSCA) conducted investigations into the murders of both President John F. Kennedy and Dr. Martin Luther King Jr. In the King case, the HSCA concluded that "there is a likelihood that James Earl Ray assassinated Dr. Martin Luther King Jr. as the result of a conspiracy" but that no U.S. government agency was part of this conspiracy.

Here are a few of the theories surrounding the assassination:

• **Man in the bushes theory:** A volunteer driver for King on his Memphis visits told police that night he ran into the street after the shot was fired and saw a man running away in the brush opposite the motel. King's closest aides interviewed by police said they saw no one in those bushes, which were directly below the second-floor rooming house where Ray was registered. U.S. Justice Department investigators later concluded what the driver probably saw were nearby police officers running toward the scene.

- **Second gun theory:** Loyd Jowers, owner of Jim's Grill, a bar located directly below the section of the rooming house where Ray was staying, claimed years later that a man came in the back door of his bar and gave him a rifle to hide. According to the Department of Justice, Jowers had inconsistently identified different people as King's assassin since 1993 and contradicted himself on virtually every key point about the alleged conspiracy.

- **CIA connection theory:** A famous photo taken on the motel balcony shows King's aides pointing in the direction from which the shot came and one man who is not pointing, but instead is kneeling over King's body. This man was an undercover cop assigned to infiltrate a black power youth group. In the initial stages of its investigation, the FBI initially hid the fact the man was an undercover cop. Later, the man would leave the Memphis police department and finish his career with the CIA. The young policeman was Marrell McCollough. He testified openly in the House Select Committee on Assassinations hearings in 1978 and said he had run up on the balcony to attempt first aid. The CIA said McCollough did not join the agency until 1974, six years after the assassination.

# AN OPEN SECRET

Was Amelia Earhart the victim of some kind of conspiracy?

Her choice not to keep up with technological know-how is more likely to blame for her disappearance.

Pioneering aviator Amelia Earhart set records and made headlines because of her talent, courage, tireless work ethic, and willingness to craft her own image. But no one is perfect, of course. Earhart failed to keep up with the technologies that helped other pilots to call for help and made flying a much less dangerous job.

## OPENING THE BOOKS

After Orville and Wilbur Wright made the first powered airplane flight in 1903, an ugly patent war began among inventors in the U.S. A huge number of researchers from all kinds of backgrounds—the Wrights themselves were bicycle mechanics, publishers, and journalists—had made incremental improvements on one another's work, brainstormed similar ideas, and generally squabbled over who was making the best progress.

These aviation pioneers went to court over fine details of one aircraft versus another, citing their own notes and evidence that had largely been kept secret. But after a decade of brutal lawsuits and public fighting over who was first, who invented what, and where the credit was due, the United States entered World War I. Aviation companies were de facto forced to pour their proprietary research and patents into a large pool shared by all of America's aircraft industry.

Making their technology "open source" was part of the war effort, but as with software and other inventions today, the open industry led to better and more rapid developments. After World War I ended, pilots began to set records left and right using ingenious inventions like the artificial horizon— something pilots still use in cockpits today, in a modernized form. And some pilots made their livings in traveling airshows as airplanes became more and more familiar, but no less mesmerizing, to the American people. Amelia Earhart was one of these pilots, traveling to build buzz for her own career.

## THE MORSE THE MERRIER

Earhart was a gifted and remarkable pilot, the first woman to ride in a plane (as a passenger) across the Atlantic and then to fly across it as the pilot. She started a professional organization for women pilots and took a faculty position at Purdue University. She and fellow groundbreaking pilot Charles Lindbergh were like movie stars by the 1930s, and Earhart was witty and engaging when she spoke with the press or members of the public. Her career was at a perfect point for her to make an outsize gesture in the form of a trip around the world. She wasn't the first, but she was definitely the most famous.

Technology leapt ahead during her career, and Morse code was in wide use by the time Earhart began her trip around the world. The world's leading navigation instructor offered to teach Earhart radio operation, Morse code, and cutting-edge navigation, but she didn't have time before her trip, which had already been delayed by a failed first attempt. The navigator she chose also didn't know Morse code. When they grew disoriented in poor weather over the Pacific Ocean, they could not call for help in Morse code, and their radio reception was too poor to send or receive verbal messages from the navy ships assigned to support the open water sections of their flight.

The "what ifs" of Earhart's failed final journey stoke pop culture across the decades, and who can say what could have happened if she and her navigator were able to get help? Without specific coordinates or landmarks, which Earhart likely could have relayed to her support team, even modern rescuers can't cover large swaths of open ocean with success. Morse code might have made the critical difference.

# WAS HITLER'S DEATH A HOAX?

Rumors of Hitler's survival persisted for years. The charred corpse was a double; he had offspring; he was living in South America, keeping that old Nazi spirit alive. Some of the wilder tales were fueled by Soviet propaganda.

They were false. In 1993 the Russian government opened the old Soviet files. We now know beyond any reasonable doubt what happened.

The NKVD (Russian intelligence) investigation began the moment Soviet troops overran the Führerbunker. They exhumed the Hitler and Goebbels bodies, bringing in close acquaintances for positive I.D.; for example, Eva and Adolf's former dentist and his assistant both recognized their own professional handiwork. The original announcement had been correct: Adolf Hitler had died April 30, 1945. After sending Hitler's jaw back to Moscow for safekeeping, the NKVD secretly reburied the other remains at a military base near Magdeburg, German Democratic Republic (East Germany).

In 1970, the Soviet military prepared to transfer the Magdeburg base to East German control. The KGB (successor to the NKVD) dared not leave the Nazi remains. On April 4, 1970, the KGB exhumed the fragmentary remains of Adolf and Eva Hitler and the Goebbels family. Hitler's skull was identified, and the bullet-holed portion was sent to Moscow. The next day, the KGB incinerated the rest of the remains, crushed them to dust and dumped it in a nearby river.

Therefore, of Eva Braun and the Goebbels family nothing at all remains. Of Hitler, today only his jaw and a skull fragment exist in Russian custody.

# PAUL IS DEAD

In the fall of 1969, a Detroit radio DJ reported that Paul McCartney, "the cute Beatle," had been killed in a car crash three years earlier and been replaced by a look-alike contest winner named William Campbell. An Eastern Michigan University student writing a review of the Beatles' latest album, Abbey Road, propelled the story, which had been floating around the rumor mill. The review claimed that many clues, collected from album covers and song lyrics, proved that McCartney was deceased (although the student admitted in a radio interview that most of his thesis was pure fabrication). Of course, the media had a field day. Radio and TV stations blared the "facts" nightly, and newspapers put their best investigative reporters on the story.

*Life* magazine devoted the cover story of a November 1969 issue to revealing the truth—McCartney was very much alive. Calling the whole story "bloody stupid," Paul hinted at something more serious—while he was full of life, the Beatles were not—claiming, "the Beatle thing is over." No one seemed to pick up on that clue—that the greatest band of the '60s would be DOA within six months.

# GONE WITHOUT A TRACE

## JIMMY HOFFA

On the afternoon of July 30, 1975, Jimmy Hoffa, former president of the International Brotherhood of Teamsters, stepped onto the parking lot of the Manchus Red Fox Restaurant near Detroit and into history. Scheduled to meet with known mobsters from New Jersey and New York, Hoffa vanished and was never seen or heard from again. Since that day, wild theories involving mob hits and political assassinations have run rampant. But despite hundreds of anonymous tips, confessions from mob hit men, and even the wife of a former mobster accusing her husband of the hit, it is still unknown what happened to Hoffa or where he's buried. The case officially remains open. As recently as 2013, FBI agents were still following leads and digging in Michigan trying to find out what happened to Hoffa.

## DOROTHY ARNOLD

After spending most of December 12, 1910, shopping in Manhattan, American socialite Dorothy Arnold told a friend she was planning to walk home through Central Park. She never made it. Fearing their daughter had eloped with her one-time boyfriend George Griscom Jr., the Arnolds immediately hired the Pinkerton Detective Agency, although they did not report her missing to police until almost a month later. Once the press heard the news, theories spread like wildfire, most of them pointing the finger at Griscom. Some believed he had murdered Arnold, but others thought she had died as the result of a botched abortion. Still others felt her family had banished her to Switzerland and then used her disappearance as a cover-up. No evidence was ever found to formally charge Griscom, and Arnold's disappearance remains unsolved.

## D. B. COOPER

On the evening of November 24, 1971, a man calling himself Dan Cooper (later known as D. B. Cooper) hijacked an airplane, and demanded $200,000 and four parachutes, which he received when the plane landed in Seattle. Cooper allowed the plane's passengers to disembark but then ordered the pilot to fly to Mexico. Once the plane had gained enough altitude, somewhere over the Cascade Mountains near Woodland, Washington, Cooper jumped from the plane and fell into history. Despite a massive manhunt, no trace of him has ever been found. In 1980, an eight-year-old boy found nearly $6,000 in rotting $20 bills lying along the banks of the Columbia River. A check of their serial numbers found that they were part of the ransom money given to Cooper, but what became of the rest of the money, and Cooper, is a mystery to this day.

# MARILYN MONROE'S DEATH

On August 5, 1962, Hollywood starlet Marilyn Monroe was found dead in her home in Brentwood, California. On the evening of August 4, she was visited by her psychiatrist, Dr. Ralph Greenson, then she made several phone calls from her bedroom, including one to actor Peter Lawford, a Kennedy family confidante.

Late that night, Monroe's housekeeper, Eunice Murray, noticed a light coming from under the actress's bedroom door, which she thought was odd. When Monroe didn't respond to her knocks, Murray went around to the side of the house and peered through the bedroom window. Monroe looked peculiar, Murray later told police, so she called Greenson, who broke into Monroe's bedroom and found her on the bed unconscious. Greenson then called Monroe's personal physician, Dr. Hyman Engelberg, who pronounced the actress dead. It was then that the police were notified.

Los Angeles Police Sgt. Jack Clemmons was the first on the scene. He said he found Monroe naked and facedown on her bed with an empty bottle of sleeping pills nearby. A variety of other pill bottles littered the nightstand.

Monroe's body was taken to Westwood Village Mortuary then transferred to the county morgue, and her house was sealed and placed under guard. Los Angeles Deputy Medical Examiner Dr. Thomas T. Noguchi performed Monroe's autopsy and concluded in his official report that the actress had died from an overdose of Nembutol (a sleeping pill) and chloral hydrate (a mild sedative) and ruled that it was a "probable suicide."

## SUICIDE, MURDER, OR ACCIDENTAL OVERDOSE?

Over the years, conspiracy theorists have had a field day with Monroe's death because of numerous inconsistencies between Noguchi's autopsy report and the evidence at the scene, as well as in the stories of those who were at the scene. Some conspiracy theorists believe that Monroe was murdered and that her death was made to look like a suicide. By who remains a mystery, though the most prevalent theory—unproved by anyone—is that the Kennedy family had her killed to avoid a scandal. However, given Monroe's habit of taking more medication than doctors prescribed, because she thought she had a high tolerance for it, accidental overdose cannot be ruled out.

# THE MYSTERIOUS DEATH OF THELMA TODD

On December 16, 1935, at about 10:30 A.M., actress Thelma Todd was found dead behind the wheel of her Lincoln Phaeton convertible. Her maid, Mae Whitehead, had come to clean the luxurious apartment Todd lived in above her rollicking roadhouse, Thelma Todd's Sidewalk Café. The maid discovered Thelma in a nearby garage. Some sources claim the ignition of her car was still turned on and the garage door was opened a crack. An obvious suicide? Not quite.

## HUMBLE BEGINNINGS

Thelma Todd was born in Lawrence, Massachusetts, on July 29, 1905 or 1906, depending on the source. She was an academically gifted girl who went on to attend college, but her mother pushed her to use her physical assets as well as her intellectual gifts. She made a name for herself in local beauty pageants, winning the title "Miss Massachusetts" in 1925. Though she did not take the top prize in the "Miss America" pageant, she was discovered by a talent agent and soon began appearing in the short one- and two-reel comedy films of producer/director Hal Roach.

Before Thelma knew it, she was starring with big names, including Gary Cooper and William Powell, and working at an exhausting pace on as many as 16 pictures a year. Her forte was comedy, however, and she found her biggest success as a sidekick to such legends as the Marx Brothers and Laurel and Hardy. Around Hollywood, she was known as "The Ice Cream Blonde" or "Hot Toddy" (a nickname she assigned to herself). But Thelma knew that fame was fleeting, and she decided to invest in a nightclub/restaurant with her sometimes boyfriend, director Roland West. The upscale gin joint became a favorite with Hollywood's hard-partying, fast set.

## A COMPLICATED GIRL

To say that Thelma's love life was messy would be an understatement. Her marriage to playboy Pasquale "Pat" DiCicco (from 1932 to 1934) was a disaster, filled with domestic abuse. She turned to West after her divorce but was reportedly also seeing mobster Charles "Lucky" Luciano on the side. It was said that Luciano wanted a room at the Sidewalk Café for his gambling operation, and he was willing to go to great lengths to get it. The rumor was that even after he got Thelma hooked on amphetamines, she was still of sound enough mind to refuse. Supposedly, the couple got into a huge screaming match about the subject one night at another restaurant, The Brown Derby, and various threats were exchanged.

## SO, WHO DID IT?

All the romantic drama and hard living came to a head on the evening of December 14, 1935. Thelma had been invited to a party involving a good friend of hers, Ida Lupino, and she was driven there by her chauffeur, Ernest Peters. Unfortunately for Thelma, her ex-husband showed up with another woman and made a scene. After a nasty argument, DiCicco left with his date, and a drunken Thelma informed Lupino that there was a new man in her life, a rich businessman from San Francisco.

Peters at dropped Thelma back at her apartment around 3:30 A.M. on December 15. She apparently couldn't get into the building and instead retreated to the garage, perhaps to sleep there. She might have turned on the car for warmth, not paying attention to the carbon monoxide. The Los Angeles County determined the time of death had been between 5:00 and 8:00 A.M.

Making the circumstances even more mysterious is the fact that, although Thelma was determined to have died early on Sunday morning, December 15, her body was not found until Monday morning. There were uncorroborated reports that she had been seen during the day on Sunday in Beverly Hills. Is it possible that Thelma actually died 24 hours later than was reported?

The coroner's report listed carbon monoxide asphyxiation as the cause of death and ruled it a suicide, but Thelma's crazy life led many to dismiss that verdict. With so many intriguing suspects—the violent ex-husband, the jealous boyfriend, the ruthless gangster lover, and the mysterious out-of-town paramour—who could blame them? That initial report was reconsidered and overturned, with the ruling changed to accidental death, but some observers believe the incident was never investigated thoroughly.

# THOMAS INCE: A BOATING EXCURSION TURNS DEADLY

Film mogul Thomas Ince joins other Hollywood notables for a weekend celebration in 1924 and ends up dead. Was it natural causes or one of the biggest cover-ups in Hollywood history?

The movie industry has been rocked by scandal throughout its history, but few incidents have matched the controversy and secrecy surrounding the death of Thomas Ince, a high-profile producer and director of many successful silent films.

During the 1910s, he set up his own studio in California where he built a sprawling complex of small homes, sweeping mansions, and other buildings that were used as sets for his movies. Known as Inceville, the studio covered several thousand acres, and it was there that Ince perfected the idea of the studio system—a factory-style setup that used a division of labor amongst large teams of costumers, carpenters, electricians, and other film professionals who moved from project to project as needed. All major Hollywood film companies would later adopt this system, which allowed for the mass production of movies with the producer in creative and financial control.

Down on his luck by the 1920s, Ince still had many influential friends and associates. In November 1924, newspaper magnate William Randolph Hearst offered to host a weekend birthday celebration for the struggling producer aboard his luxury yacht the *Oneida*. Several Hollywood luminaries attended, including Charlie Chaplin and Marion Davies, as well Louella Parsons, then a junior writer for one of Hearst's East Coast newspapers. But at the end of the cruise, Ince was carried off the ship on a medical gurney and rushed home, where he died two days later. A hastily scribbled death certificate blamed heart failure.

## THE RUMORS FLY

Almost immediately, the rumor mill churned out shocking and sordid versions of the incident, which were very different from the official line. A Chaplin employee, who was waiting at the docks when the boat returned, reportedly claimed that Ince was suffering from a gunshot wound to the head when he was taken off the *Oneida*. Could he have been the victim of a careless accident at the hands of a partying Hollywood celeb? Perhaps, but film industry insiders knew of complex and passionate relationships among those on board, and a convoluted and bizarre scenario soon emerged and has persisted to this day. As it turns out, Davies was Hearst's longtime mistress, despite being almost 34 years his junior. She was also a close friend of the notorious womanizer Chaplin. Many speculate that Hearst, enraged over the attention that Chaplin was paying to the young ingénue, set out to kill him but shot the hapless Ince by mistake.

Certain events after Ince's death helped the rumors gain traction. Ince's body was cremated, so no autopsy could be performed. And his grieving widow was whisked off to Europe for several months courtesy of Hearst—conveniently away from the reach of the American press. Louella Parsons was also elevated within the Hearst organization, gaining a lifetime contract and the plum assignment as his number-one celebrity gossip columnist, which she parlayed into a notoriously self-serving enterprise. Conspiracy theorists believe that she wrangled the deal with Hearst to buy her silence about the true cause of Ince's death.

## LINGERING MYSTERY

Was Ince the victim of an errant gunshot and subsequent cover-up? If anyone in 1920s California had the power to hush witnesses and bend officials to his will in order to get

away from murder, it was the super rich and powerful Hearst. But no clear evidence of foul play has emerged after all these decades. Still, the story has persisted and even served as the subject for *The Cat's Meow*, a 2002 film directed by Peter Bogdanovich, which starred Kirsten Dunst as Davies and Cary Elwes as the doomed Ince.

# WHAT REALLY KILLED JOHN WAYNE?

*The Conqueror* (1956) wasn't exactly John Wayne's masterpiece. According to "The Duke" himself, the film was actually written with Marlon Brando in mind for the lead role, and this historical drama has been criticized for miscasting Wayne in the part. However, *The Conqueror* has been connected to far worse things than box-office failure: Some say the movie is to blame for Wayne's death from stomach cancer two decades after its debut. What's more, Wayne isn't the only person believed to have died as a result of the project. Was the nearby nuclear testing site to blame?

## RADIATION EXPOSURE

The questions surrounding *The Conqueror* come as a result of its filming location: The movie was shot near St. George and Snow Canyon, Utah, an area in the vicinity of a nuclear testing site. In the early 1950s, the U.S. military set off nearly a dozen atomic bombs just miles away from the location, sending clouds of radioactive dust into St. George and Snow Canyon. Work on *The Conqueror* began just two years later, even though the film company and cast knew about the radiation. To make matters worse, after the location work had wrapped, the film's crew transported dirt from the area back to soundstages in Hollywood to help re-create the setting for in-studio shooting. (At the time, the effects of radiation exposure were not as well documented as they are today.)

In the years following the filming of *The Conqueror*, numerous members of the cast and crew developed cancer. Aside from Wayne, at least 45 people from the group died from causes related to the disease, including actress Agnes Moorehead, who died in 1974 from uterine cancer; actress

Susan Hayward, who died from brain and skin cancer at age 57 in 1975; and director Dick Powell, who, in 1963, passed away at age 58 from lymphatic cancer. Actors Pedro Armendariz and John Hoyt both took their own lives after learning of their diagnoses.

An article published in *People* magazine in 1980 stated that 41 percent of those who worked on the movie—91 out of 220 people—later developed cancer. That figure reportedly didn't include the hundreds of Utah-based actors who worked as extras. Still, the numbers far exceeded any statistical normality for a given group of individuals. A scientist with the Pentagon's Defense Nuclear Agency was quoted in the article as saying: "Please, God, don't let us have killed John Wayne."

## BROADER FINDINGS

While many of the actors were heavy smokers—Wayne included—the strange circumstances surrounding the filming of *The Conqueror* have turned into an underground scandal of sorts. And the general findings from the city of St. George certainly don't help quell the concerns.

In 1997, a study by the National Cancer Institute found that children who lived in the St. George area during the 1950s were exposed to as much as 70 times the amount of radiation than was originally reported because of contaminated milk taken from exposed animals. Consequently, the study reported that the children had elevated risks for cancer development. The report further stated that the government "knew from the beginning that a Western test site would spread contamination across most of the country" and that the exposure could have easily been avoided.

The government eventually passed an act called the Radiation Exposure Compensation Act, which provided $50,000 to people who lived downwind of the nuclear testing site near St. George and had been exposed to radiation. At least 40,000 people are thought to have been exposed in Utah alone. While John Wayne is the most famous of them, the true cause of his cancer may never be definitively known.

# BLACK DAHLIA MURDER MYSTERY

One of the most baffling murder mysteries in U.S. history began innocently enough on the morning of January 15, 1947. Betty Bersinger was walking with her young daughter in the Leimert Park area of Los Angeles, when she spotted something lying in a vacant lot that caused her blood to run cold. She ran to a nearby house and called the police. Officers Wayne Fitzgerald and Frank Perkins arrived on the scene shortly after 11:00 A.M.

## A GRISLY DISCOVERY

Lying only several feet from the road, in plain sight, was the naked body of a young woman. Her body had numerous cuts and abrasions, including a knife wound from ear to ear that resembled a ghoulish grin. Even more horrific was that her body had been completely severed at the midsection, and the two halves had been placed as if they were part of some morbid display. That's what disturbed officers the most: The killer appeared to have carefully posed the victim close to the street because he wanted people to find his grotesque handiwork.

Something else that troubled the officers was that even

though the body had been brutally violated and desecrated, there was very little blood found at the scene. The only blood evidence recovered was a possible bloody footprint and an empty cement package with a spot of blood on it. In fact, the body was so clean that it appeared to have just been washed.

Shortly before removing the body, officers scoured the area for a possible murder weapon, but none was recovered. A coroner later determined that the cause of death was from hemorrhage and shock due to a concussion of the brain and lacerations of the face, probably from a very large knife.

## POSITIVE IDENTIFICATION

After a brief investigation, police were able to identify the deceased as Elizabeth Short, who was born in Hyde Park, Massachusetts, on July 29, 1924. At age 19, Short had moved to California to live with her father, but she moved out and spent the next few years moving back and forth between California, Florida, and Massachusetts. In July 1946, Short returned to California to see Lt. Gordon Fickling, a former boyfriend, who was stationed in Long Beach. For the last six months of her life, Short lived in an assortment of hotels, rooming houses, and private homes. She was last seen a week before her body was found, which made police very interested in finding out where and with whom she spent her final days.

## THE BLACK DAHLIA IS BORN

As police continued their investigation, reporters jumped all over the story and began referring to the unknown killer by names such as "sex-crazed maniac" and even "werewolf." Short herself was also given a nickname: the Black Dahlia. Reporters said it was a name friends had called her as a play on the movie *The Blue Dahlia*, which had recently been released. However, others contend Short was never called the Black Dahlia while she was alive; it was just something reporters made up for a better story. Either way, it wasn't long before newspapers around the globe were splashing front-page headlines about the horrific murder of the Black Dahlia.

## THE KILLER IS STILL OUT THERE

As time wore on, hundreds of police officers were assigned to the Black Dahlia investigation. They combed the streets, interviewing people and following leads. Although police interviewed thousands of potential suspects—and dozens even confessed to the murder—to this day, no one has ever officially been charged with the crime. More than 60 years and several books and movies after the crime, the Elizabeth Short murder case is still listed as "open." We are no closer to knowing who killed Short or why than when her body was first discovered.

There is one bright note to this story. In February 1947, perhaps as a result of the Black Dahlia case, the state of California became the first state to pass a law requiring all convicted sex offenders to register themselves.

# YOU BIG FAKERS!

Celebrities are known to do weird things—bark crazy demands, shave their head, throw objects at their employees, or—in extreme cases—fake his (or her) own death. Granted, sometimes it's not the celeb's fault— enduring fans often simply refuse to let their heroes die. Here are some stories of celebrities whose obituaries may or may not be false.

## ELVIS PRESLEY

Elvis might have left the building, but many of his devoted fans believe he is still among the living. Despite reports of his death at Graceland on August 16, 1977, some believe Presley had grown weary of the star lifestyle and just wanted out.

However, death doesn't mean The King hasn't been making the rounds. Presley is one of the most impersonated singers in the world, which makes it hard to determine whether sightings of the singer are indeed real. The first sighting reportedly occurred just hours after Presley's death was announced, when a man by the name of John Burrows paid cash for a one-way ticket to Buenos Aires—and the name John Burrows was one of the aliases that Presley often used. Today, more than 40 years after his death, there are still regularly reported Presley sightings.

## JIM MORRISON

Starting as early as 1967, The Doors' snakelike singer, Jim Morrison, was talking about possibly faking his own death and starting anew in Africa. He even invented an alter ego, Mr. Mojo Risin' (an anagram of his name). So when he was found dead in a bathtub in Paris, France, on July 3, 1971, some people had their doubts. Rumors were fueled by the fact that in the time it took his parents, family, and friends to get to Paris, Morrison's body was already sealed inside a coffin. Upon seeing Morrison's gravesite, Doors drummer John Densmore is said to have remarked that the grave was too short.

The first two years after Morrison's death were when he was most often spotted. In 1973, he was even reportedly spotted inside the Bank of America in San Francisco conducting business. But as time went on, the sightings eventually stopped, leaving all of us to scratch our heads and wonder if and when Morrison finally decided to break on through to the other side.

## WELDON KEES

Even as tourists are snapping away taking photographs of the iconic Golden Gate Bridge in San Francisco, few are aware of its dark side. Since 1937, more than 1,280 individuals are known to have committed suicide by jumping from the bridge—a number that more than likely is higher because some bodies are never recovered. So on July 19, 1955, when the car belonging to author Weldon Kees was found on the north end of the Golden Gate Bridge, keys still in the ignition, most believed he had become another sad statistic. Friends reported that Kees had been depressed; he had even telephoned his friend Janet Richards to tell her, "things are pretty bad here."

Yet there seemed to be something staged about the whole scene at the Golden Gate Bridge. It seemed too perfect. After friends searched his apartment and discovered that items such as his wallet, savings account book, and sleeping bag were missing, it was thought that Kees might have faked his own death. Perhaps he was depressed with the way his life had turned out and was looking to reinvent himself. A possible clue lies in one of the things Kees said to Richards the day before he disappeared: "I may go to Mexico. To stay."

## ALAN ABEL

On January 2, 1980, both the *New York Times* and the *New York Daily News* published an obituary for author and satirist

Alan Abel, stating that he had died of a heart attack while skiing at a Utah resort.

There was only one problem—Abel was still alive. The following day, Abel held a press conference to declare the whole thing an elaborate hoax. Abel said he had spent more than six months plotting out the specifics of the clever ruse, including having an actor stop by the ski resort claiming to be a funeral director who needed to collect Abel's belongings. Abel also had a woman pretend to be his widow and contact the newspapers to verify his death. Years later, a mutual friend introduced Abel to an aspiring actor and comedian that was fascinated with Abel's death hoax: Andy Kaufman.

## ANDY KAUFMAN

Whether it was proclaiming himself the holder of a nonexistent wrestling title or staging fistfights on live national television, Kaufman loved nothing better than to pull a fast one. So when it was announced on May 16, 1984, that Kaufman, a nonsmoker, had passed away at age 35, a mere five months after being diagnosed with a rare form of lung cancer, people couldn't help but think it was his latest stunt. Even Kaufman's close friend and sometime coconspirator Bob Zmuda had his doubts, especially since Kaufman had previously said that he was considering faking his own death. In the years following his death, there were several reports of Kaufman making appearances in nightclubs disguised as one of his alter egos, Tony Clifton.

On May 16, 2004, the 20th anniversary of Kaufman's death, Zmuda and some of Andy's closest friends threw a "Welcome Home" party and patiently waited for Andy to crash it. Unfortunately, he never showed.

# WILLIAM DESMOND TAYLOR

The murder of actor/director William Desmond Taylor was like something out of an Agatha Christie novel, complete with a handsome, debonair victim and multiple suspects, each with a motive. But unlike Christie's novels, in which the murderer was always unmasked, Taylor's death remains unsolved nearly 100 years later.

On the evening of February 1, 1922, Taylor was shot in the back by an unknown assailant; his body was discovered the next morning by a servant, Henry Peavey. News of Taylor's demise spread quickly, and several individuals, including officials from Paramount Studios, where Taylor was employed, raced to the dead man's home to clear it of anything incriminating, such as illegal liquor, evidence of drug use, illicit correspondence, and signs of sexual indiscretion. However, no one called the police until later in the morning.

## NUMEROUS SUSPECTS

Soon an eclectic array of potential suspects came to light, including Taylor's criminally inclined former butler, Edward F. Sands, who had gone missing before the murder; popular movie comedienne Mabel Normand, whom Taylor had entertained the evening of his death; actress Mary Miles Minter, who had a passionate crush on the handsome director who was 28 years her senior; and Charlotte Shelby, Minter's mother, who often wielded a gun to protect her daughter's tarnished honor.

Taylor's murder was the last thing Hollywood needed at the time, coming as it did on the heels of rape allegations against popular film comedian Fatty Arbuckle. Scandals brought undue attention on Hollywood, and the Arbuckle story had taken its toll. Officials at Paramount tried to keep a lid on the Taylor story, but the tabloid press had a field day. A variety of personal foibles were made public in the weeks that followed, and both Normand and Minter saw their careers come to a screeching halt as a result. Taylor's own indiscretions were also revealed, such as the fact that he kept a special souvenir, usually lingerie, from every woman he bedded.

## LITTLE EVIDENCE

Police interviewed many of Taylor's friends and colleagues, including all potential suspects. However, there was no evidence to incriminate anyone specifically, and no one was formally charged.

Investigators and amateur sleuths pursued the case for years. Sands was long a prime suspect, based on his criminal past and his estrangement from the victim. But it was later revealed that on the day of the murder, Sands had signed in for work at a lumberyard in Oakland, California— some 400 miles away—and thus could not have committed the crime. Coming in second was Shelby, whose temper and threats were legendary. Shelby's own acting career had fizzled out early, and all of her hopes for stardom were pinned on her daughter. She threatened many men who tried to woo Mary.

In the mid-1990s, another possible suspect surfaced—a long-forgotten silent-film actress named Margaret Gibson. According to Bruce Long, author of *William Desmond Taylor: A Dossier*, Gibson confessed to a friend on her deathbed in 1964 that years before she had killed a man named William Desmond Taylor. However, the woman to whom Gibson cleared her conscience didn't know who Taylor was and thought nothing more about it.

## THE MYSTERY CONTINUES

Could Margaret Gibson (aka Pat Lewis) be Taylor's murderer? She had acted with Taylor in Hollywood in the early 1910s, and she may even have been one of his many sexual conquests. She also had a criminal past, including charges of blackmail, drug use, and prostitution, so it's entirely conceivable that she was a member of a group trying to extort money from the director, a popular theory among investigators. But according to an earlier book, *A Cast of Killers* by Sidney D. Kirkpatrick, veteran Hollywood director King Vidor had investigated the murder as material for a film script and through his research believed Shelby was the murderer. But out of respect for Minter, he never did anything about it.

Ultimately, however, we may never know for certain who killed William Desmond Taylor, or why. The case has long grown cold, and anyone with specific knowledge of the murder is likely dead. Unlike a Hollywood thriller, in which the killer is revealed at the end, Taylor's death is a macabre puzzle that likely will never be solved.

# THE DEATH OF JOHN DILLINGER...OR SOMEONE WHO LOOKED LIKE HIM

On July 22, 1934, outside the Biograph Theater on Chicago's north side, John Dillinger, America's first Public Enemy Number One, passed from this world into the next in a hail of bullets. Or did he? Conspiracy theorists believe that FBI agents shot and killed the wrong man and covered it all up when they realized their mistake. So what really happened that night? Let's first take a look at the main players in this gangland soap opera.

## HOOVER WANTS HIS MAN

Born June 22, 1903, John Dillinger was in his early thirties when he first caught the FBI's eye. They thought they were through with him in January 1934, when he was arrested after shooting a police officer during a bank robbery in East Chicago, Indiana. However, Dillinger managed to stage a daring escape from his Indiana jail cell using a wooden gun painted with black shoe polish.

Once Dillinger left Indiana in a stolen vehicle and crossed into Illinois, he was officially a federal fugitive. J. Edgar Hoover, then director of the FBI, promised a quick apprehension, but Dillinger had other plans. He seemed to enjoy the fact that the FBI was tracking him—rather than go into hiding, he continued robbing banks. Annoyed, Hoover assigned FBI Agent Melvin Purvis to ambush Dillinger. Purvis's plan backfired, though, and Dillinger escaped, shooting and killing two innocent men in the process. After the botched trap, the public was in an uproar and the FBI was under close scrutiny. To everyone at the FBI, the message was clear: Hoover wanted Dillinger, and he wanted him ASAP.

## THE WOMAN IN RED

The FBI's big break came in July 1934 with a phone call from a woman named Anna Sage. Sage was a Romanian immigrant who ran a Chicago-area brothel. Fearing that she might be deported, Sage wanted to strike a bargain with the feds. Her proposal was simple: In exchange for not being deported, Sage was willing to give the FBI John Dillinger. According to Sage, Dillinger was dating Polly Hamilton, one of her former employees. Melvin Purvis personally met with Sage and told her he couldn't make any promises but he would do what he could about her pending deportation.

Several days later, on July 22, Sage called the FBI office in Chicago and said that she was going to the movies that night with Dillinger and Hamilton. Sage quickly hung up but not before saying she would wear something bright so that agents could pick out the threesome in a crowd. Not knowing which movie theater they were planning to go to, Purvis dispatched several agents to the Marbro Theater, while he and another group of agents went to the Biograph. At approximately 8:30 P.M., Purvis believed he saw Dillinger, Sage, and Hamilton enter the Biograph. As she had promised, Sage indeed wore something bright—an orange blouse. However, under the marquee lights, the blouse's color appeared to be red, which is why Sage was forever dubbed "The Woman in Red."

Purvis tried to apprehend Dillinger right after he purchased tickets, but he slipped past Purvis and into the darkened theater. Purvis went into the theater but was unable to locate Dillinger in the dark. At that point, Purvis left the theater, gathered his men, and made the decision to apprehend Dillinger as he was exiting the theater. Purvis positioned himself in the theater's vestibule, instructed his men to hide outside, and told them that he would signal them by lighting a cigar when he spotted Dillinger. That was their cue to move in and arrest Dillinger.

## "STICK 'EM UP, JOHNNY!"

At approximately 10:30 P.M., the doors to the Biograph opened and people started to exit. All of the agents' eyes were on Purvis. When a man wearing a straw hat, accompanied by two women, walked past Purvis, the agent quickly placed a cigar in his mouth and lit a match. Perhaps sensing something was wrong, the man turned and looked at Purvis, at which point Purvis drew his pistol and said,

"Stick 'em up, Johnny!" In response, the man turned as if he was going to run away, while at the same time reaching for what appeared to be a gun. Seeing the movement, the other agents opened fire. As the man ran away, attempting to flee down the alleyway alongside the theater, he was shot four times on his left side and once in the back of the neck before crumpling on the pavement. When Purvis reached him and checked for vitals, there were none. Minutes later, after being driven to a local hospital, John Dillinger was pronounced DOA. But as soon as it was announced that Dillinger was dead, the controversy began.

## DILLINGER DISPUTED

Much of the basis for the conspiracy stems from the fact that Hoover, both publicly and privately, made it clear that no matter what, he wanted Dillinger caught. On top of that, Agent Purvis was under a lot of pressure to capture Dillinger, especially since he'd failed with a previous attempt. Keeping that in mind, it would be easy to conclude that Purvis, in his haste to capture Dillinger, might have overlooked a few things. First, it was Purvis alone who pointed out the man he thought to be Dillinger to the waiting agents. Conspiracy theorists contend that Purvis fingered the wrong man that night, and an innocent man ended up getting killed as a result. As evidence, they point to Purvis's own statement: While they were standing at close range, the man tried to pull a gun, which is why the agents had to open fire. But even though agents stated they recovered a .38-caliber Colt automatic from the victim's body (and even displayed it for many years), author Jay Robert Nash discovered that that particular model was not even available until five months after Dillinger's alleged death. Theorists believe that when agents realized they'd not only shot the wrong man, but an unarmed one at that, they planted the gun as part of a cover-up.

Another interesting fact that could have resulted in Purvis's misidentification was that Dillinger had recently undergone plastic surgery in an attempt to disguise himself. In addition to work on his face, Dillinger had attempted to obliterate his fingerprints by dipping his fingers into an acid solution. On top of that, the man who Purvis said was Dillinger was wearing a straw hat the entire time Purvis saw him. It is certainly possible that Purvis did not actually recognize Dillinger but instead picked out someone who merely looked like him. If you remember, the only tip Purvis had was Sage telling him that she was going to the movies with Dillinger and his girlfriend. Did Purvis see Sage leaving the theater in her orange blouse and finger the wrong man simply because he was standing next to Sage and resembled Dillinger? Or was the whole thing a setup orchestrated by Sage and Dillinger to trick the FBI into executing an innocent man?

## SO WHO WAS IT?

If the man shot and killed outside the theater wasn't John Dillinger, who was it? There are conflicting accounts, but one speculation is that it was a man named Jimmy Lawrence, who was dating Polly Hamilton. If you believe in the conspiracy, Lawrence was simply in the wrong place at the wrong time. Or possibly, Dillinger purposely sent Lawrence to the theater hoping FBI agents would shoot him, allowing Dillinger to fade into obscurity. Of course, those who don't believe in the conspiracy say the reason Lawrence looked so much like Dillinger is because he was Dillinger using an alias. Further, Dillinger's sister, Audrey Hancock, identified his body. Finally, they say it all boils down to the FBI losing or misplacing the gun Dillinger had the night he was killed and inadvertently replacing it with the wrong one. Case closed.

Not really, though. It seems that whenever someone

comes up with a piece of evidence to fuel the conspiracy theory, someone else has something to refute it. Some have asked that Dillinger's body be exhumed and DNA tests be performed, but nothing has come of it yet. Until that happens, we'll probably never know for sure what really happened on that hot July night back in 1934.

# OHIO'S GREATEST UNSOLVED MYSTERY

From 1935 until 1938, a brutal madman roamed the Flats of Cleveland. The killer—known as the Mad Butcher of Kingsbury Run—is believed to have murdered 12 men and women. Despite a massive manhunt, the murderer was never apprehended.

In 1935, the Depression had hit Cleveland hard, leaving large numbers of people homeless. Shantytowns sprang up on the eastern side of the city in Kingsbury Run—a popular place for transients—near the Erie and Nickel Plate railroads.

It is unclear who the Butcher's first victim was. Recent research suggests it may have been an unidentified woman found floating in Lake Erie—in pieces—on September 5, 1934; she would be known as Jane Doe I but dubbed by some as the "Lady of the Lake." The first official victim was found in the Jackass Hill area of Kingsbury Run on September 23, 1935. The unidentified body, labeled John Doe, had been dead for almost a month. A mere 30 feet away from the body was another victim, Edward Andrassy. Unlike John Doe, Andrassy had only been dead for days, indicating that the spot was a dumping ground. Police began staking out the area.

After a few months passed without another body, police thought the worst was over. Then on January 26, 1936, the partial remains of a new victim, a woman, were found in downtown Cleveland. On February 7, more remains were found at a separate location, and the deceased was identified as Florence Genevieve Polillo. Despite similarities among the three murders, authorities had yet to connect them—serial killers were highly uncommon at the time.

## TATTOO MAN, ELIOT NESS, AND MORE VICTIMS

On June 5, two young boys passing through Kingsbury Run discovered a severed head. The rest of the body was found near the Nickel Plate railroad police station. Despite six distinctive tattoos on the man's body (thus the nickname "Tattoo Man"), he was never identified and became John Doe II.

At this point, Cleveland's newly appointed director of public safety, Eliot Ness, was officially briefed on the case. While Ness and his men hunted down leads, the headless body of another unidentified male was found west of Cleveland on July 22, 1936. It appeared that the man, John Doe III, had been murdered several months earlier. On September 10, the headless body of a sixth victim, John Doe IV, was found in Kingsbury Run.

Ness officially started spearheading the investigation. Determined to bring the killer to justice, Ness's staff fanned out across the city, even going undercover in the Kingsbury Run area. As 1936 drew to a close, no suspects had been named or new victims discovered. City residents believed that Ness's team had run the killer off. But future events would prove that the killer was back...with a vengeance.

# THE BODY COUNT CLIMBS

A woman's mutilated torso washed up on the beach at 156th Street on February 23, 1937. The rest would wash ashore two months later. (Strangely, the body washed up in the same location as the "Lady of the Lake" had three years earlier.)

On June 6, 1937, teenager Russell Lauyer found the decomposed body of a woman inside of a burlap sack under the Lorain-Carnegie Bridge in Cleveland. With the body was a newspaper from June of the previous year, suggesting a timeline for the murder. An investigation indicated the body might belong to one Rose Wallace; this was never confirmed, and the victim is sometimes referred to as Jane Doe II. Pieces of another man's body (the ninth victim) began washing ashore on July 6, just below Kingsbury Run. Cleveland newspapers were having a field day with the case that the "great" Eliot Ness couldn't solve. This fueled Ness, and he promised justice.

# BURNING OF KINGSBURY RUN

The next nine months were quiet, and the public began to relax. When a woman's severed leg was found in the Cuyahoga River on April 8, 1938, however, people debated its connection to the Butcher. But the rest of Jane Doe III was soon found inside two burlap sacks floating in the river (sans head, of course).

On August 16, 1938, the last two confirmed victims of the Butcher were found together at the East 9th Street Lakeshore Dump. Jane Doe IV had apparently been dead for four to six months prior to discovery, while John Doe VI may have been dead for almost nine months.

Something snapped inside Eliot Ness. On the night of August 18, Ness and dozens of police officials raided the shantytowns in the Flats, ending up in Kingsbury Run. Along the way, they interrogated or arrested anyone they came across, and Ness ordered the shanties burned to the ground. There would be no more confirmed victims of the Mad Butcher of Kingsbury Run.

## WHO WAS THE MAD BUTCHER?

There were two prime suspects in the case, though no one was ever charged. The first was Dr. Francis Sweeney, a surgeon with the knowledge many believed necessary to mutilate the victims the way the killer did. (He was also a cousin of Congressman Martin L. Sweeney, a known political opponent of Ness.)

In August 1938, Dr. Sweeney was interrogated by Ness, two other men, and the inventor of the polygraph machine, Dr. Royal Grossman. By all accounts, Sweeney failed the polygraph test (several times), and Ness believed he had his man, but he was released due to lack of evidence. Two days after the interrogation, on August 25, 1938, Sweeney checked himself into the Sandusky Veterans Hospital. He remained institutionalized at various facilities until his death in 1965. Because Sweeney voluntarily checked himself in, he could have left whenever he desired.

The other suspect was Frank Dolezal, who was arrested by private investigators on July 5, 1939, as a suspect in the murder of Florence Polillo, with whom he had lived for a time. While in custody, Dolezal confessed to killing Polillo, although some believe the confession was forced. Either way, Dolezal died under mysterious circumstances while incarcerated at the Cuyahoga County Jail before he could be charged.

As for Eliot Ness, some believe his inability to bring the Butcher to trial weighed on him for the rest of his life. Ness went to his grave without getting a conviction. To this day, the case remains open.

# ANYTHING BUT SPLENDOR: NATALIE WOOD

The official account of Natalie Wood's tragic death is riddled with holes. For this reason, cover-up theorists continue to run hog-wild with conjecture. Here's a sampling of the questions, facts, and assertions surrounding the case.

## A LIFE IN PICTURES

There are those who will forever recall Natalie Wood as the adorable child actress from *Miracle on 34th Street* (1947) and those who remember her as the sexy but wholesome grown-up star of movies such as *West Side Story* (1961), *Splendor in the Grass* (1961), and *Bob & Carol & Ted & Alice* (1969). Both groups generally agree that Wood had uncommon beauty and talent.

Wood appeared in her first film, *Happy Land* (1943), in a bit part alongside other people from her hometown of Santa Rosa, California, where the film was shot. She stood out to the director, who remembered her later when he needed to cast a child in another film. Wood was uncommonly mature and professional for a child actress, which helped her make a relatively smooth transition to ingénue roles.

Although Wood befriended James Dean and Sal Mineo— her troubled young costars from *Rebel Without a Cause* (1955)—and she briefly dated Elvis Presley, she preferred to move in established Hollywood circles. By the time she was 20, she was married to Robert Wagner and was costarring with Frank Sinatra in *Kings Go Forth* (1958), which firmly ensconced her in the Hollywood establishment. The early 1960s represent the high point of Wood's career, and she specialized in playing high-spirited characters with determination and spunk. She added two more Oscar nominations to the one she received for *Rebel* and racked up five Golden Globe nominations for Best Actress. This period also proved to be personally turbulent for Wood, as she suffered through a failed marriage to Wagner and another to Richard Gregson. After taking time off to raise her children, she remarried Wagner and returned to her acting career.

## SHOCKING NEWS

And so, on November 29, 1981, the headline hit the newswires much like an out-of-control car hits a brick wall. Natalie Wood, the beautiful, vivacious 43-year-old star of stage and screen, had drowned after falling from her yacht the *Splendour*, which was anchored off California's Santa Catalina Island. Wood had been on the boat during a break from her latest film, *Brainstorm*, and was accompanied by Wagner and *Brainstorm* costar Christopher Walken. Skipper Dennis Davern was at the helm. Foul play was not suspected.

## IN MY ESTEEMED OPINION

After a short investigation, Chief Medical Examiner Dr. Thomas Noguchi listed Wood's death as an accidental drowning. Tests revealed that she had consumed "seven or eight" glasses of wine, and the coroner contended that in her intoxicated state Wood had probably stumbled and fallen overboard while attempting to untie the yacht's rubber dinghy. He also stated that cuts and bruises on her body could have occurred when she fell from the boat.

## DOUBTING THOMASES

To this day, many question Wood's mysterious demise and believe that the accidental drowning theory sounds a bit too convenient. Pointed questions have led to many rumors: Does someone know more about Wood's final moments than they're letting on? Was her drowning really an accident, or did someone intentionally or accidentally help her overboard? Could this be why she sustained substantial bruising on her face and the back of her legs? Why was Wagner so reluctant to publicly discuss the incident? Were Christopher Walken and Wood an item as had been rumored? With this possibility in mind, could a booze-fueled fight have erupted between the two men? Could Wood have then tried to intervene, only to be knocked overboard for her efforts? And why did authorities declare Wood's death accidental so quickly? Would such a hasty ruling have been issued had the principals not been famous, wealthy, and influential?

## RIPPLES

At the time of Wood's death, she and Wagner were seven years into their second marriage to each other. Whether Wood was carrying on an affair with Walken, as was alleged, may be immaterial, even if it made for interesting tabloid fodder. But Wagner's perception of their relationship could certainly be a factor. If nothing else, it might better explain the argument that ensued between Wagner and Walken that fateful night.

## CASE CLOSED?

Further information about Wood's death is sparse because no eyewitnesses have come forward. However, a businesswoman whose boat was anchored nearby testified that she heard a woman shouting for help, and then a voice responding, "We'll be over to get you," so the woman went back to bed. Just after dawn, Wood's body was found floating a mile away from the *Splendour*, approximately 200 yards offshore. The dinghy was found nearby; its only cargo was a stack of lifejackets.

In 2008, after 27 years of silence, Robert Wagner recalled in his autobiography, *Pieces of My Heart: A Life*, that he and Walken had engaged in a heated argument during supper after Walken had suggested that Wood star in more films, effectively keeping her away from their children. Wagner and Walken then headed topside to cool down. Sometime around midnight, Wagner said he returned to his cabin and discovered that his wife was missing. He soon realized that the yacht's dinghy was gone as well. In his book, he surmised that Wood may have gone to secure the dinghy that had been noisily slapping against the boat. Then, tipsy from the wine, she probably fell into the ocean and drowned. Walken notified the authorities.

Was Natalie Wood's demise the result of a deadly mix of wine and saltwater as the coroner's report suggests? This certainly could be the case. But why would she leave her warm cabin to tend to a loose rubber dinghy in the dark of night? Could an errant rubber boat really make such a commotion?

Perhaps we'll never know what happened that fateful night, but an interview conducted shortly before Wood's death proved prophetic: "I'm frightened to death of the water," said Wood about a long-held fear. "I can swim a little bit, but I'm afraid of water that is dark."

# FAMOUS UFO SIGHTINGS

Whatever you call them, unidentified flying objects, foo fighters, or ghost rockets, strange objects in the sky remain one of the world's truly mysterious phenomena. Here are some of the most famous UFO sightings.

## THE BATTLE OF LOS ANGELES

On February 25, 1942, just weeks after Japan's attack on Pearl Harbor and America's entry into World War II, late-night air-raid sirens sounded a blackout order throughout Los Angeles County in California. A silvery object (or objects) was spotted in the sky, prompting an all-out assault from ground troops. For a solid hour, antiaircraft fire bombarded the unidentified craft with some 1,400 shells, as numerous high-powered searchlights followed its slow movement across the sky. Several witnesses reported direct hits on the invader, though it was never downed. After the "all clear" was sounded, the object vanished, and it has never been identified.

## THE MARFA LIGHTS

The town of Marfa, located far out in western Texas, is home to what many believe is the best concentration of "ghost lights" in the nation. Almost nightly, witnesses along Highway 67 can peer across the flatland north of the Chinati Mountains and spot glowing orbs of varying color and size, bobbing and floating among the brush. It's an event that's reportedly been witnessed since the 1880s. Though several scientists have conducted studies, no one has been able to determine their origin. Nevertheless, local officials have capitalized on the phenomenon and constructed an official roadside viewing area.

## THE WASHINGTON FLAP

In two separate incidents just days apart in 1952, numerous objects were detected high above Washington, D.C., moving erratically at speeds as fast as 7,000 miles per hour. At one point, separate military radar stations detected the same objects simultaneously. Several eyewitnesses viewed the objects from the ground and from air control towers, and three pilots spotted them at close range, saying they looked like the lit end of a cigarette or like falling stars without tails. The official air force explanation was "temperature inversion," and the sightings were labeled "unexplained."

## THE HILL ABDUCTION, AKA THE ZETA RETICULI INCIDENT

By the 1960s, a number of people had reportedly seen UFOs but hadn't actually encountered aliens personally. But on September 19, 1961, Barney and Betty Hill found themselves being chased by a spacecraft along Route 3 in New Hampshire. The object eventually descended upon their vehicle, whereupon Barney witnessed several humanoid creatures through the craft's windows. The couple tried to escape, but their car began shaking violently, and they were forced off the road. Suffering lapses in memory from that moment on, the Hills later recalled being taken aboard the ship, examined, and questioned by figures with very large eyes. Only locals and the UFO community knew the incident until the 1966 publication of *The Interrupted Journey* by John Fuller.

## THE APOLLO 11 TRANSMISSION

When American astronauts made that great leap onto the surface of the moon on July 20, 1969, they apparently weren't alone. Although the incident has been repeatedly denied, believers point to a transmission from the lunar surface that had been censored by NASA but was reportedly picked up by private ham-radio operators: "These babies are huge, sir! Enormous!… You wouldn't believe it. I'm telling you there are other spacecraft out there, lined up on the far side of the crater edge. They're on the moon watching us!"

## FIRE IN THE SKY

After completing a job along Arizona's Mogollon Rim on November 5, 1979, Travis Walton and six fellow loggers spotted a large spacecraft hovering near the dark forest road leading home. Walton approached the craft on foot and was knocked to the ground by a beam of light. Then he and the craft disappeared. Five days later, Walton mysteriously reappeared just outside of town. He said that during his time aboard the spacecraft, he had struggled to escape from the short, large-headed creatures that performed experiments on his body. Neither Walton nor any of his coworkers has strayed from the facts of their stories in nearly 40 years.

## JAPAN AIRLINES FLIGHT 1628

On November 17, 1986, as Japan Airlines flight 1628 passed over Alaska, military radar detected an object on its tail. When the blip caught up with the cargo jet, the pilot reported seeing three large craft shaped like shelled walnuts, one of which was twice the size of an aircraft carrier. The objects matched the airplane's speed and tracked it for nearly an hour. At one point, the two smaller craft came so close that the pilot said he could feel their heat. The incident prompted an official FAA investigation and made worldwide headlines.

## THE PHOENIX LIGHTS

In March 1997, hundreds, if not thousands, of witnesses throughout Phoenix, Arizona, and the surrounding area caught sight of what was to become the most controversial UFO sighting in decades. For at least two hours, Arizona residents watched an array of lights move across the sky, and many reportedly saw a dark, triangular object between them. The lights, which varied in color, were even caught on videotape. Nearby military personnel tried to reproduce the event by dropping flares from the sky, but most witnesses weren't satisfied with what was deemed a diversion from the truth.

## ROSWELL

Undoubtedly the most famous UFO-related location, Roswell immediately brings to mind flying-saucer debris, men in black, secret military programs, alien autopsies, weather balloons, and government cover-ups. The incident that started it all occurred during the first week of July 1947, just before Roswell Army Air Field spokespersons claimed they had recovered parts of a wrecked "flying disc" from a nearby ranch. The report was quickly corrected to involve a weather balloon instead, which many insist was part of a cover-up. In later years, people claiming to have been involved in the recovery effort began to reveal insider information, insisting that not only was the wreckage of extraterrestrial origin, but that autopsies had been performed on alien bodies recovered from the site. Ever since, the name of this small New Mexico town has been synonymous with ufology, making Roswell a popular stop for anyone interested in all things alien.

# MESSAGES FROM MARS?

Rumors of life on Mars have been a common trope in 20th century entertainment, but nothing is getting Martian enthusiasts more excited than NASA's *Curiosity* rover that landed on the red planet in 2012. It has been six years since the rover landed to explore, analyze, and collect compounds, rocks, and atmosphere samples on the planet to determine the possibilities of life. But who's to say that Mars isn't already supporting life?

The rover's right-side navigation camera (navcam) captured a bright speck that flared upward toward the sky as the rover worked its way into new Martian territory, known as Kimberly. The web-master for the paranormal news site UFO Sighting Daily, Scott C. Waring, has taken great interest in the photo and what it might mean for life on Mars. He speculates that the speck of light could be a signal from Martians that live under the planet's surface, or, he concedes, it could be a data dropout from the video's transmission back to Earth.

The only hiccup in the extraterrestrial hypothesis is that the rover's navcam system works in stereo and the left-side camera did not pick up the flash of light that was shown from the right side. This could be a major indicator that what was seen was just a data dropout, but the news has many enthusiasts watching. Whether or not Martians are sending up flares from their subterranean abodes is unknown, but with the help of enthusiasts, all of the information sent back from the rover will continue to be scrupulously examined and questioned for any signs of life.

# THE PASCAGOULA ABDUCTION

It was around 10:30 P.M. on October 11, 1973, when Charles Hickson and Calvin Parker showed up at the Jackson County Sheriff's Office in Pascagoula, Mississippi. There had been a frantic-sounding call from a phone booth earlier in the evening and one of the deputies on duty told them to come in. The report they wanted to make wasn't the kind of thing they could easily make over the phone.

Smelling liquor on Hickson's breath, Sheriff Diamond suspected at first that it was all just a drunken prank. Parker wasn't a drinker though, and Hickson said he had needed a belt of whiskey to calm his nerves after what had happened earlier in the evening. And if any of it was true, not too many people would blame him for it.

Despite the sheriff's skepticism, they related their story.

The two men had been fishing off a dock on the Pascagoula River around 9:00 P.M. It was a quiet spot near the old abandoned Shaupeter Shipyard. Hickson had caught redfish and speckled trout there before, and they were hoping for better fishing than they had had earlier in the evening. Then they saw the light.

It appeared in the sky not too far from them—maybe 30 yards or so away. It was bright and blue and a quiet buzzing sound came with it. It circled around and they realized as it came down in a clearing nearby that it was a solid object, perhaps 30 feet long and 10 feet high and shaped like a football. Both men were terrified. For a moment it just hovered there, two or three feet off the ground. And then the object opened up, revealing a brilliantly lit interior.

Three creatures emerged from the ship. Each one was about five feet tall, and could be generously described as humanoid. They had gray skin, and neckless heads with cones jutting out where the ears and nose should be. If they had eyes, they were lost in the wrinkles of their flesh. Instead of typical feet, their legs ended in stumps, and instead of hands they had claws like a lobster or a crab. They floated towards Hickson and Parker.

Hickson found himself unable to move when two of the creatures gently scooped him up in their claws and spirited him into the craft. Parker fainted, understandably given the circumstances, and was brought over by the third being. Once aboard, Hickson was examined by an eye-shaped probe moving around him while feeling paralyzed. His panicked attempts to communicate were met with buzzing sounds from the creatures. Eventually he was left alone, still unable to move. After about 20 minutes, it was over. In his initial recounting of the incident, Hickson couldn't describe how he got back on the shore; he just remembered seeing Parker, standing there in a state of shock. They heard the telltale buzzing sound from before, and the ship departed.

Once they got bearings, they stopped and called the nearest Air Force base. The person on the other end of the line told them the Air Force wasn't in the business of collecting reports like that anymore and that they should contact the local authorities. Fearing they would be laughed off but still wanting to tell some authority about the experience, they tried the local paper, only to find the offices closed for the evening. It was then that they called the sheriff's office.

After running them through the story a few times, the sheriff left them alone without letting them know they were being recorded. At this point, he still suspected it might all be some elaborate ruse. But instead of dropping the act and maybe snickering about pulling one over on the police as he suspected they would, Hickson and Parker commiserated.

The experience seemed to have rattled them terribly. Neither of them could get over just how strange the encounter had been. Parker wanted to see a doctor. Hickson wondered if they'd ever be believed. When Hickson left the room a few minutes later, Parker broke down and started praying.

Eventually, the men left for home after getting assurances that there wouldn't be any publicity. It was clear even the next day, however, that the story had leaked, apparently from someone in the sheriff's office. It was ultimately investigated by Dr. Allen Hynek, who was still attached to the Air Force's Project Blue Book, and James Harder, a professor of civil and hydraulic engineering at University of California–Berkley who had testified before the U.S. House of Representatives Committee on Science and Aeronautics about UFOs back in 1968. Hynek and Harder were both convinced something truly strange had happened to the two men that night by the Pascagoula River.

The case received quite a bit of media attention, culminating with an appearance on the *Dick Cavette Show* for Hickson. Neither of the men tried to use the experience to make real money, however. Over time it became apparent that other people had seen strange things in the sky near Pascagoula that night, although not necessarily the same distinctive blue light.

The abduction changed both men's lives forever, if in different ways. Charles Hickson, although initially troubled by nightmares after the incident, came to speak about it freely, appeared on the lecture circuit, and eventually self-published a book about what had happened. He remained eager to share his experience until his death in September of 2011 at the age of 80. Perhaps the way he dealt with it all was informed by one of the small differences in their accounts: Hickson claimed that before leaving, the beings telepathically communicated to him that they had come in peace. Parker experienced no such comforting coda. According to one newspaper article, Parker expressed his suspicion that the creatures may have been demons. "I'm a firm believer in God," he was quoted as saying many years later, "and where there's good, there's bad." The stress eventually led to a nervous breakdown, and he's been only sporadically involved with the UFO community. After years spent working in the oil industry out west, he eventually moved back to the area. As of 2013, he sometimes went fishing not too far from the riverbank where so many years before his world was turned upside down.

# THE KECKSBURG INCIDENT

Did visitors from outer space once land in a western Pennsylvania thicket?

## DROPPING IN FOR A VISIT

On December 9, 1965, an unidentified flying object (UFO) streaked through the late-afternoon sky and landed in Kecksburg—a rural Pennsylvania community about 40 miles southeast of Pittsburgh. This much is not disputed. However, specific accounts vary widely from person to person. Even after closely examining the facts, many people remain undecided about exactly what happened. "Roswell" type incidents—ultra-mysterious in nature and reeking of a governmental cover-up—have an uncanny way of causing confusion.

## TRAJECTORY-INTERRUPTUS

A meteor on a collision course with Earth will generally "bounce" as it enters the atmosphere. This occurs due to friction, which forcefully slows the average space rock from 6 to 45 miles per second to a few hundred miles per hour, the speed at which it strikes Earth and officially becomes a meteorite. According to the official explanation offered by the U.S. Air Force, it was a meteorite that landed in Kecksburg. However, witnesses reported that the object completed back and forth maneuvers before landing at a very low speed— moves that an unpowered chunk of earthbound rock simply cannot perform. Strike one against the meteor theory.

## AN ACORN-SHAPE METEORITE?

When a meteor manages to pierce Earth's atmosphere, it has the physical properties of exactly what it is: a space rock. That is to say, it will generally be unevenly shaped, rough, and darkish in color, much like rocks found on Earth. But at Kecksburg, eyewitnesses reported seeing something far, far different. The unusual object they described was bronze to golden in color, acorn-shape, and as large as a Volkswagen Beetle automobile. Unless the universe has started to produce uniformly shaped and colored meteorites, the official explanation seems highly unlikely. Strike two for the meteor theory.

## MARKEDLY DIFFERENT

Then there's the baffling issue of markings. A meteorite can be chock-full of holes, cracks, and other such surface imperfections. It can also vary somewhat in color. But it should never, ever have markings that seem intelligently designed. Witnesses at Kecksburg describe intricate writings similar to Egyptian hieroglyphics located near the base of the object. A cursory examination of space rocks at any natural history museum reveals that such a thing doesn't occur naturally. Strike three for the meteor theory. Logically following such a trail, could an unnatural force have been responsible for the item witnessed at Kecksburg? At least one man thought so.

## REPORTIS RIGOR MORTIS

Just after the Kecksburg UFO landed, reporter John Murphy arrived at the scene. Like any seasoned pro, the newsman immediately snapped photos and gathered eyewitness accounts of the event. Strangely, FBI agents arrived, cordoned off the area, and confiscated all but one roll of his film. Undaunted, Murphy assembled a radio documentary entitled *Object in the Woods* to describe his experience. Just before the special was to air, the reporter received an unexpected visit by two men. According to a fellow employee, a dark-suited pair identified themselves as government agents and subsequently confiscated a portion of Murphy's audiotapes. A week later, a clearly perturbed Murphy aired a watered-down version of his documentary. In it, he claimed that certain interviewees requested their accounts be removed for fear of retribution at the hands of police, military, and government officials. In 1969, John Murphy was struck dead by an unidentified car while crossing the street.

## RESURRECTED BY ROBERT STACK

In all likelihood the Kecksburg incident would have remained dormant and under-explored had it not been for the television show *Unsolved Mysteries*. In a 1990 segment, narrator Robert Stack took an in-depth look at what occurred in Kecksburg, feeding a firestorm of interest that eventually brought forth two new witnesses. The first, a U.S. Air Force officer stationed at Lockbourne AFB (near Columbus, Ohio), claimed to have seen a flatbed truck carrying a mysterious object as it arrived on base on December 10, 1965. The military man told of a tarpaulin-covered conical object that he couldn't identify and a "shoot to kill" order given to him for anyone who ventured too close. He was told that the truck was bound for Wright-Patterson AFB in Dayton, Ohio, an installation that's alleged to contain downed flying saucers. The other witness was a building contractor who claimed to have delivered 6,500 special bricks to a hangar inside Wright-Patterson AFB on December 12, 1965. Curious, he peeked inside the hangar and saw a "bell-shaped" device, 12 feet high, surrounded by several men wearing anti-radiation style suits. Upon leaving, he was told that he had just witnessed an object that would become "common knowledge" in the next 20 years.

## WILL WE EVER KNOW THE TRUTH?

Like Roswell before it, we will probably never know for certain what occurred in western Pennsylvania back in 1965. The more that's learned about the case, the more confusing and contradictory it becomes. For instance, the official 1965 meteorite explanation contains more holes than Bonnie and Clyde's death car, and other explanations, such as orbiting space debris (from past U.S. and Russian missions) reentering Earth's atmosphere, seem equally preposterous. In 2005, as the result of a new investigation launched by the Sci-Fi Television Network, NASA asserted that the object was a Russian satellite. According to a NASA spokesperson, documents of this investigation were somehow misplaced in the 1990s. Mysteriously, this finding directly contradicts the official air force version that nothing at all was found at the Kecksburg site. It also runs counter to a 2003 report made by NASA's own Nicholas L. Johnson, Chief Scientist for Orbital Debris. That document shows no missing satellites at the time of the incident. This includes a missing Russian Venus Probe (since accounted for)—the very item that was once considered a prime crash candidate.

## BRAVE NEW WORLD

These days, visitors to Kecksburg will be hard-pressed to find any trace of the encounter—perhaps that's how it should be. Since speculation comes to an abrupt halt whenever a concrete answer is provided, Kecksburg's reputation as "Roswell of the East" looks secure, at least for the foreseeable future. But if one longs for proof that something mysterious occurred there, they need look no further than the backyard of the Kecksburg Volunteer Fire Department. There, in all of its acorn-shape glory, stands an full-scale mock-up of the spacecraft reportedly found in this peaceful town on December 9, 1965. There too rests the mystery, intrigue, and romance that have accompanied this alleged space traveler for more than 40 years.

# TO THE MOON!

Television and film star Jackie Gleason was fascinated with the paranormal and UFOs. But he had no idea that an innocent game with an influential friend would lead him face-to-face with his obsession.

Jackie Gleason was a star of the highest order. The rotund actor kept television audiences in stitches with his portrayal of hardheaded but ultimately lovable family man Ralph Kramden in the 1955 sitcom *The Honeymooners*. He made history with his regularly aimed, but never delivered, threats to TV wife Alice, played by Audrey Meadows: "One of these days Alice, one of these days, pow, right in the kisser," and "Bang, zoom! To the moon, Alice!"

But many fans didn't know that Gleason was obsessed with the supernatural, and he owned a massive collection of memorabilia on the subject. It was so large and impressive that the University of Miami, Florida, put it on permanent exhibit after his death in 1987. He even had a house built in the shape of a UFO, which he christened, "The Mothership." The obsession was legendary, and it climaxed in an unimaginable way.

## A HIGH STAKES GAME

An avid golfer, Gleason also kept a home close to Inverrary Golf and Country Club in Lauderhill, Florida. A famous golfing buddy lived nearby—U.S. President Richard M. Nixon, who had a compound on nearby Biscayne Bay. The Hollywood star and the controversial politician shared a love of the links, politics, and much more.

The odyssey began when Gleason and Nixon met for a golf tournament at Inverrary in February 1973. Late in the day their conversation turned to a topic close to Gleason's heart—UFOs. To the funnyman's surprise, the president revealed his own fascination with the subject, touting a large collection of books that rivaled Gleason's. They talked shop through the rest of the game, but Gleason noticed reservation in Nixon's tone, as if the aides and security within earshot kept the president from speaking his mind. He would soon learn why.

Later that evening around midnight, an unexpected guest visited the Gleason home. It was Nixon, alone. The customary Secret Service detail assigned to him was nowhere to be seen. Confused, Gleason asked Nixon the reason for such a late call. He replied only that he had to show Gleason something. They climbed into Nixon's private car and sped off. The drive brought them to Homestead Air Force Base in South Miami-Dade County. Nixon took them to a large, heavily guarded building. Guards parted as the pair headed inside the structure, Gleason following Nixon past labs before arriving at a series of large cases. The cases held wreckage from a downed UFO, Nixon told his friend. Seeing all of this, Gleason had his doubts and imagined himself the target of an elaborated staged hoax.

Leaving the wreckage, the pair entered a chamber holding six (some reports say eight) freezers topped with thick glass. Peering into the hulls, Gleason later said he saw dead bodies—but not of the human variety. The remains were small, almost childlike in stature, but withered in appearance and possessing only three or four digits per hand. They were also severely mangled, as if they had been in a devastating accident.

Returning home, Gleason was giddy. His obsession had come full circle. The enthusiasm changed in the weeks that followed, however, shifting to intense fear and worry. A patriotic American, Gleason couldn't reconcile his government's secrecy about the UFO wreckage. Traumatized, he began drinking heavily and suffered from severe insomnia.

## THE "TRUTH" COMES OUT

Gleason kept details of his wild night with Nixon under wraps. Unfortunately, his soon-to-be-ex-wife didn't follow his lead. Beverly Gleason spilled the beans in *Esquire* magazine and again in an unpublished memoir on her marriage to Gleason. Supermarket tabloids ate the story up.

Gleason only opened up about his night with Nixon in the last weeks of his life. Speaking to Larry Warren, a former air force pilot with his own UFO close encounter, a slightly boozy Gleason let his secret loose with a phrase reminiscent of his *Honeymooners* days: "We've got 'em...Aliens!"

# THE MYSTERIOUS ORB

If Texas were a dartboard, the city of Brownwood would be at the center of the bull's-eye. Maybe that's how aliens saw it, too.

Brownwood is a peaceful little city with about 20,000 residents and a popular train museum. A frontier town at one time, it became the trade center of Texas when the railroad arrived in 1885. Since then, the city has maintained a peaceful lifestyle. Even the massive tornado that struck Brownwood in 1976 left no fatalities. The place just has that "small town" kind of feeling.

## AN INVADER FROM THE SKY

In July 2002, however, the city's peace was broken. Brownwood made international headlines when a strange metal orb fell from space, landed in the Colorado River, and washed up just south of town. The orb looked like a battered metal soccer ball—it was about a foot across, and it weighed just under ten pounds. Experts described it as a titanium sphere. When it was x-rayed, it revealed a second, inner sphere with tubes and wires wrapped inside.

That's all that anybody knows (or claims to know). No one is sure what the object is, and no one has claimed responsibility for it. The leading theory is that it's a cryogenic tank from some kind of spacecraft from Earth, used to store a small amount of liquid hydrogen or helium for cooling purposes. Others have speculated that it's a bomb, a spying device, or even a weapon used to combat UFOs.

## IT'S NOT ALONE

The Brownwood sphere isn't unique. A similar object landed in Kingsbury, Texas, in 1997, and was quickly confiscated by the air force for "tests and analysis." So far, no further announcements have been made.

Of course, the air force probably has a lot to keep it busy. About 200 UFOs are reported each month, and Texas is among the top three states where UFOs are seen. But until anything is known for sure, those in Texas at night should keep an eye on the skies.

# UNIDENTIFIED SUBMERGED OBJECTS

Much like their flying brethren, unidentified submerged objects captivate and mystify. But instead of vanishing into the skies, USOs, such as the following, plunge underwater.

## SIGHTING AT PUERTO RICO TRENCH

In 1963, while conducting exercises off the coast of Puerto Rico, U.S. Navy submarines encountered something extraordinary. The incident began when a sonar operator aboard an accompanying destroyer reported a strange occurrence. According to the seaman, one of the subs traveling with the armada broke free from the pack to chase a USO. This quarry would be unlike anything the submariners had ever pursued.

Underwater technology in the early 1960s was advancing

rapidly. Still, vessels had their limitations. The U.S.S. *Nautilus*, though faster than any submarine that preceded it, was still limited to about 20 knots (23 miles per hour). The bathyscaphe *Trieste*, a deep-sea submersible, could exceed 30,000 feet in depth, but the descent took as long as five hours. Once there, the vessel could not be maneuvered side to side.

Knowing this, the submariners were stunned by what they witnessed. The USO was moving at 150 knots (170 miles per hour) and hitting depths greater than 20,000 feet! No underwater vehicles on Earth were capable of such fantastic numbers. Even today, modern nuclear subs have top speeds of about 25 knots (29 miles per hour) and can operate at around 800-plus feet below the surface.

Thirteen separate crafts witnessed the USO as it crisscrossed the Atlantic Ocean over a four-day period. At its deepest, the mystery vehicle reached 27,000 feet. To this day, there's been no earthly explanation offered for the occurrence.

## USO WITH A BUS PASS

In 1964, London bus driver Bob Fall witnessed one of the strangest USO sightings. While transporting a full contingent of passengers, the driver and his fares reported seeing a silver, cigar-shape object dive into the nearby waters of the River Lea. The police attributed the phenomenon to a flight of ducks, despite the obvious incongruence. Severed telephone lines and a large gouge on the river's embankment suggested something far different.

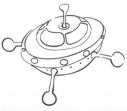

## PASCAGOULA INCIDENT

On November 6, 1973, at approximately 8:00 P.M., a USO was sighted by at least nine fishermen anchored off the coast of Pascagoula, Mississippi. They witnessed an underwater object an estimated five feet in diameter that emitted a strange amber light.

First to spot the USO was Rayme Ryan. He repeatedly poked at the light-emitting object with an oar. Each time he made contact with the strange object, its light would dim and it would move a few feet away, and then brighten once again.

Fascinated by the ethereal quality of this submerged question mark, Ryan summoned the others. For the next half hour, the cat-and-mouse game played out in front of the fishermen until Ryan struck the object with a particularly forceful blow. With this action, the USO disappeared from view.

The anglers moved about a half-mile away and continued fishing. After about 30 minutes, they returned to their earlier location and were astounded to find that the USO had returned. At this point, they decided to alert the coast guard.

After interviewing the witnesses, investigators from the Naval Ship Research and Development Laboratory in Panama City, Florida, submitted their findings: At least nine persons had witnessed an undetermined light source whose characteristics and actions were inconsistent with those of known marine organisms or with an uncontrolled human-made object. Their final report was inconclusive, stating that the object could not be positively identified.

# JOHN LENNON SEES A UFO

Lucy in the sky with warp drive.

In May 1974, former Beatle John Lennon and his assistant/ mistress May Pang returned to New York City after almost a year's stay in Los Angeles, a period to which Lennon would later refer as his "Lost Weekend." The pair moved into Penthouse Tower B at 434 East 52nd Street. As Lennon watched television on a hot summer night, he noticed flashing lights reflected in the glass of an open door that led onto a patio. At first dismissing it as a neon sign, Lennon suddenly realized that since the apartment was on the roof, the glass couldn't be reflecting light from the street. So— sans clothing—he ventured onto the terrace to investigate. What he witnessed has never been satisfactorily explained.

## SPEECHLESS

As Pang recollected, Lennon excitedly called for her to come outside. Pang did so. "I looked up and stopped mid-sentence," she said later. "I couldn't even speak because I saw this thing up there...it was silvery, and it was flying very slowly. There was a white light shining around the rim and a red light on the top...[it] was silent. We started to watch it drift down, tilt slightly, and it was flying below rooftops. It was the most amazing sight." She quickly ran back into the apartment, grabbed her camera, and returned to the patio, clicking away.

Lennon friend and rock photography legend Bob Gruen picked up the story: "In those days, you didn't have answering machines, but a service [staffed by people], and I had received a call from 'Dr. Winston.'" (Lennon's original middle name was Winston, and he often used the alias "Dr. Winston O'Boogie.") When Gruen returned the call,

Lennon explained his incredible sighting and insisted that the photographer come round to pick up and develop the film personally. "He was serious," Gruen said. "He wouldn't call me in the middle of the night to joke around." Gruen noted that although Lennon had been known to partake in mind-altering substances in the past, during this period he was totally straight. So was Pang, a nondrinker who never took drugs and whom Gruen characterized as "a clear-headed young woman."

The film in Pang's camera was a unique type supplied by Gruen, "four times as fast as the highest speed then [commercially] available." Gruen had been using this specialty film, usually employed for military reconnaissance, in low-light situations such as recording studios. The same roll already had photos of Lennon and former bandmate Ringo Starr, taken by Pang in Las Vegas during a recording session.

Gruen asked Lennon if he'd reported his sighting to the authorities. "Yeah, like I'm going to call the police and say I'm John Lennon and I've seen a flying saucer," the musician scoffed. Gruen picked up the couple's phone and contacted the police, the *Daily News*, and the *New York Times*. The photographer claims that the cops and the *News* admitted that they'd heard similar reports, while the *Times* just hung up on him.

## IT WOULD HAVE BEEN THE ULTIMATE TRIP

Gruen's most amusing recollection of Lennon, who had been hollering "UFO!" and "Take me with you!" was that none of his NYC neighbors either saw or heard the naked, ex-Beatle screaming from his penthouse terrace. And disappointingly, no one who might have piloted the craft responded to Lennon's pleas.

Gruen took the exposed film home to process, "sandwiching" it between two rolls of his own. Gruen's negatives came out perfectly, but the film Pang shot was "like a clear plastic strip," Gruen says. "We were all baffled... that it was completely blank."

Lennon remained convinced of what he'd seen. In several shots from a subsequent photo session with Gruen that produced the iconic shot of the musician wearing a New York City T-shirt (a gift from the photographer), John points to where he'd spotted the craft. And on his Walls and Bridges album, Lennon wrote in the liner notes: "On the 23rd Aug. 1974 at 9 o'clock I saw a U.F.O.—J.L."

Who's to say he and May Pang didn't? Certainly not Gruen, who still declares—more than 35 years after the fact—"I believed them."

And so the mystery remains.

## THE GREAT TEXAS AIRSHIP MYSTERY

Roswell, New Mexico, may be the most famous potential UFO crash site, but did Texas experience a similar event in the 19th century?

A UFO crashed in Aurora, Texas, one sunny April morning in 1897.

Six years before the Wright Brothers' first flight and 50 years before Roswell, a huge, cigar-shape UFO was seen in the skies. It was first noted on November 17, 1896, about a thousand feet above rooftops in Sacramento, California. From there, the spaceship traveled to San Francisco, where it was seen by hundreds of people.

## A NATIONAL TOUR

Next, the craft crossed the United States, where thousands observed it. Near Omaha, Nebraska, a farmer reported the ship on the ground, making repairs. When it returned to the skies, it headed toward Chicago, where it was photographed on April 11, 1897, the first UFO photo on record. On April 15, near Kalamazoo, Michigan, residents reported loud noises "like that of heavy ordnance" coming from the spaceship.

Two days later, the UFO attempted a landing in Aurora, Texas, which should have been a good place. The town was almost deserted, and its broad, empty fields could have been an ideal landing strip.

## NO SMOOTH SAILING

However, at about 6:00 A.M. on April 17, the huge, cigar-shape airship "sailed over the public square and, when it reached the north part of town, collided with the tower of Judge Proctor's windmill and went to pieces with a terrific explosion, scattering debris over several acres of ground, wrecking the windmill and water tank and destroying the judge's flower garden."

That's how Aurora resident and cotton buyer S. E. Haydon described the events for *The Dallas Morning News*. The remains of the ship seemed to be strips and shards of a silver-colored metal. Just one body was recovered. The newspaper reported, "while his remains are badly disfigured, enough of the original has been picked up to show that he was not an inhabitant of this world."

On April 18, reportedly, that body was given a good, Christian burial in the Aurora cemetery, where it may remain to this day. A 1973 effort to exhume the body and examine it was successfully blocked by the Aurora Cemetery Association.

## A FIRSTHAND ACCOUNT

Although many people have claimed the Aurora incident was a hoax, an elderly woman was interviewed in 1973 and clearly recalled the crash from her childhood. She said that her parents wouldn't let her near the debris from the spacecraft, in case it contained something dangerous. However, she described the alien as "a small man."

Aurora continues to attract people interested in UFOs. They wonder why modern Aurora appears to be laid out like a military base. Nearby, Fort Worth seems to be home to the U.S. government's experts in alien technology. Immediately after the Roswell UFO crash in 1947, debris from that spaceship was sent to Fort Worth for analysis.

## IS THERE ANY TRACE LEFT?

*The Aurora Encounter*, a 1986 movie, documents the events that began when people saw the spacecraft attempt a landing at Judge Proctor's farm. Today, the Oates gas station marks the area where the UFO crashed. Metal debris was collected from the site in the 1970s and studied by North Texas State University. That study called one fragment "most intriguing": It appeared to be iron but wasn't magnetic; it was shiny and malleable rather than brittle, as iron should be.

As recently as 2008, UFOs have appeared in the north central Texas skies. In Stephenville, a freight company owner and pilot described a low-flying object in the sky, "a mile long and half a mile wide." Others who saw the ship several times during January 2008 said that its lights changed configuration, so it wasn't an airplane. The government declined to comment.

Today, a plaque at the Aurora cemetery mentions the spaceship, but the alien's tombstone—which, if it actually existed, is said to have featured a carved image of a spaceship—was stolen many years ago.

# IT'S A BIRD! IT'S A PLANE! IT'S... AVROCAR?!?

Not all UFOs are alien spaceships. One top-secret program was contracted out by the U.S. military to an aircraft company in Canada.

Oh, the 1950s—a time of sock hops, drive-in movies, and the Cold War between America and the Soviet Union, when each superpower waged war against the other in the arenas of scientific technology, astronomy, and politics. It was also a time when discussion of life on other planets was rampant, fueled by the alleged crash of an alien spaceship near Roswell, New Mexico, in 1947.

## WATCH THE SKIES

Speculation abounded about the unidentified flying objects (UFOs) spotted nearly every week by everyone from farmers to airplane pilots. As time passed, government authorities began to wonder if the flying saucers were, in fact, part of a secret Russian program to create a new type of air force. Fearful that such a craft would upset the existing balance of power, the U.S. Air Force decided to produce its own saucer-shape ship.

In 1953, the military contacted Avro Aircraft Limited of Canada, an aircraft manufacturing company that operated in Malton, Ontario, between 1945 and 1962. Project Silverbug was initially proposed simply because the government wanted to find out if UFOs could be manufactured by humans. But before long, both the military and the scientific community were speculating about its potential. Intrigued by the idea, designers at Avro—led by British aeronautical engineer John Frost—began working on the VZ-9-AV Avrocar. The round craft would have been right at home in a scene from the classic science fiction film *The Day the Earth Stood Still*. Security for the project was so tight that it probably generated rumors that America was actually testing a captured alien spacecraft—speculation that remains alive and well even today.

## OF THIS EARTH

By 1958, the company had produced two prototypes, which were 18 feet in diameter and 3.5 feet tall. Constructed around a large triangle, the Avrocar was shaped like a disk, with a curved upper surface. It included an enclosed 124-blade turbo-rotor at the center of the triangle, which provided lifting power through an opening in the bottom of the craft. The turbo also powered the craft's controls. Although conceived as being able to carry two passengers, in reality a single pilot could barely fit inside the cramped space. The Avrocar was operated with a single control stick, which activated different panels around the ship. Airflow issued from a large center ring, which was controlled by the pilot to guide the craft either vertically or horizontally.

The military envisioned using the craft as "flying Jeeps" that would hover close to the ground and move at a maximum speed of 40 miles per hour. But that, apparently, was only going to be the beginning. Avro had its own plans, which included not just commercial Avrocars, but also a family-size Avrowagon, an Avrotruck for larger loads, Avroangel to rush people to the hospital, and a military Avropelican, which, like a pelican hunting for fish, would conduct surveillance for submarines.

## BUT DOES IT FLY?

The prototypes impressed the U.S. Army enough to award Avro a $2 million contract. Unfortunately, the Avrocar project was canceled when an economic downturn forced the company to temporarily close and restructure. When Avro Aircraft reopened, the original team of designers had dispersed. Further efforts to revive the project were unsuccessful, and repeated testing proved that the craft was inherently unstable. It soon became apparent that whatever UFOs were spotted overhead, it was unlikely that they came from this planet. Project Silverbug was abandoned when funding ran out in March 1961, but one of the two Avrocar prototypes is housed at the U.S. Army Transportation Museum in Fort Eustis, Virginia.

# CELEBRITY UFO SIGHTINGS

## GORDON COOPER

Astronaut Gordon Cooper participated in a United Nations panel discussion on UFOs in New York in 1985. In the discussion, Cooper said, "I believe that these extraterrestrial vehicles and their crews are visiting this planet from other planets, which obviously are a little more technically advanced than we are here on Earth. I feel that we need to have a top-level, coordinated program to scientifically collect and analyze data from all over the Earth concerning any type of encounter, and to determine how best to interface with these visitors in a friendly fashion."

## MUHAMMAD ALI

Heavyweight boxing champ Muhammad Ali claimed to have seen UFOs hovering over New York City. The occurrence was said to have taken place early in his career while he was working with his trainer, Angelo Dundee, in Central Park. Just before dawn, the two men observed a large, round UFO as it came out from behind the city skyline and moved slowly across the sky, a sighting that lasted about 15 minutes. Ali claimed at least 16 sightings. In one, he was a passenger in a car motoring along the New Jersey Turnpike when a cigar-shape craft hovered briefly over his vehicle.

## RONALD REAGAN

Former actor and U.S. President Ronald Reagan witnessed UFOs on two occasions. Once during his term as California governor (1967–1975), Reagan and his wife Nancy arrived late to a party hosted by actor William Holden. Guests including Steve Allen and Lucille Ball reported that the couple excitedly described how they had just witnessed a UFO while driving along the Pacific Coast Highway. They had stopped to watch the event, which made them late to the party.

Reagan also confessed to a *Wall Street Journal* reporter that in 1974, when the gubernatorial jet was preparing to land in Bakersfield, California, he noticed a strange bright light in the sky. The pilot followed the light for a short time before it suddenly shot up vertically at a high rate of speed and disappeared from sight. Reagan stopped short of labeling the light a UFO, of course. As actress Lucille Ball said in reference to Reagan's first alleged UFO sighting, "After he was elected president, I kept thinking about that event and wondered if he still would have won if he told everyone that he saw a flying saucer."

## JIMI HENDRIX

Guitarist Jimi Hendrix often claimed to have been followed around by UFOs and frequently referred to them in his lyrics. In addition, Hendrix allegedly was saved from freezing to death in 1965 by an eight-foot-tall angel-like alien who thawed the snowdrift in which the musician's van was stuck. He also once told a *New York Times* reporter that he was actually from Mars.

## JIMMY CARTER

During Jimmy Carter's presidential election campaign of 1976, he told reporters that he once saw what could have been a UFO in 1969, before he was governor of Georgia. "It was the darndest thing I've ever seen," he said of the incident. He claimed that the object that he and a group of others had watched for ten minutes was as bright as the moon. Carter was often referred to as "the UFO president" after being elected because he filed a report on the matter.

## DAVID DUCHOVNY

In 1982, long before he starred as a believer in the supernatural on the hit sci-fi series *The X-Files*, David Duchovny thought he saw a UFO. Although, by his own admission, he's reluctant to say with any certainty that it wasn't something he simply imagined as a result of stress and overwork. "There was something in the air and it was gone," he later told reporters. "I thought: 'You've got to get some rest, David.'"

## WILLIAM SHATNER

For decades, the man who played Captain Kirk in the original *Star Trek* series claimed that an alien saved his life. When the actor and a group of friends were riding their motorbikes through the desert in the late 1960s, Shatner was inadvertently left behind when his bike wouldn't restart after driving into a giant pothole. Shatner said that he spotted an alien in a silver suit standing on a ridge and that it led him to a gas station and safety. Shatner later stated in his autobiography, *Up Till Now*, that he made up the part about the alien during a television interview.

# STRANGE LIGHTS IN MARFA

If anyone is near Marfa at night, they should watch for odd, vivid lights over nearby Mitchell Flat. Many people believe that the lights from UFOs or even alien entities can be seen. The famous Marfa Lights are about the size of basketballs and are usually white, orange, red, or yellow. These unexplained lights only appear at night and usually hover above the ground at about shoulder height. Some of the lights—alone or in pairs—drift and fly around the landscape.

From cowboys to truck drivers, people traveling in Texas near the intersection of U.S. Route 90 and U.S. Route 67 in southwest Texas have reported the Marfa Lights. And these baffling lights don't just appear on the ground. Pilots and airline passengers claim to have seen the Marfa Lights from the skies. So far, no one has proved a natural explanation for the floating orbs.

## EYEWITNESS INFORMATION

Two 1988 reports were especially graphic. Pilot R. Weidig was about 8,000 feet above Marfa when he saw the lights and estimated them rising several hundred feet above the ground. Passenger E. Halsell described the lights as larger than the plane and noted that they were pulsating. In 2002, pilot B. Eubanks provided a similar report.

In addition to what can be seen, the Marfa Lights may also trigger low-frequency electromagnetic (radio) waves—which can be heard on special receivers—similar to the "whistlers" caused by lightning. However, unlike such waves from power lines and electrical storms, the Marfa whistlers are extremely loud. They can be heard as the orbs appear, and then they fade when the lights do.

## A LITTLE BIT ABOUT MARFA

Marfa is about 60 miles north of the Mexican border and about 190 miles southeast of El Paso. This small, friendly Texas town is 4,800 feet above sea level and covers 1.6 square miles.

In 1883, Marfa was a railroad water stop. It received its name from the wife of the president of the Texas and New Orleans Railroad, who chose the name from a Russian novel that she was reading. A strong argument can be made that this was Dostoyevsky's *The Brothers Karamazov*. The town grew slowly, reaching its peak during World War II when the U.S. government located a prisoner of war camp, the Marfa Army Airfield, and a chemical warfare brigade nearby. (Some skeptics suggest that discarded chemicals may be causing the Marfa Lights, but searchers have found no evidence of such.)

Today, Marfa is home to nealy 2,000 people. The small town is an emerging arts center with more than a dozen artists' studios and art galleries. However, Marfa remains most famous for its light display. The annual Marfa Lights Festival is one of the town's biggest events, but the mysterious lights attract visitors year-round.

The Marfa Lights are seen almost every clear night, but they never manifest during the daytime. The lights appear between Marfa and nearby Paisano Pass, with the Chinati Mountains as a backdrop.

## WIDESPREAD SIGHTINGS

The first documented sighting was by 16-year-old cowhand Robert Reed Ellison during an 1883 cattle drive. Seeing an odd light in the area, Ellison thought he'd seen an Apache campfire. When he told his story in town, however, settlers told him that they'd seen lights in the area, too, and they'd never found evidence of campfires.

Two years later, 38-year-old Joe Humphreys and his wife, Sally, also reported unexplained lights at Marfa. In 1919, cowboys on a cattle drive paused to search the area for the origin of the lights. Like the others, they found no explanation for what they had seen.

In 1943, the Marfa Lights came to national attention when Fritz Kahl, an airman at the Marfa Army Base, reported that airmen were seeing lights that they couldn't explain. Four years later, he attempted to fly after them in a plane but came up empty again.

## EXPLANATIONS?

Some skeptics claim that the lights are headlights from U.S. 67, dismissing the many reports from before cars—or U.S. 67—were in the Marfa area. Others insist that the lights are swamp gas, ball lightning, reflections off mica deposits, or a nightly mirage.

At the other extreme, a contingent of people believe that the floating orbs are friendly observers of life on Earth. For example, Mrs. W. T. Giddings described her father's early 20th-century encounter with the Marfa Lights. He'd become lost during a blizzard, and according to his daughter, the lights "spoke" to him and led him to a cave where he found shelter.

Most studies of the phenomenon, however, conclude that the lights are indeed real but cannot be explained. The 1989 TV show *Unsolved Mysteries* set up equipment to find an explanation. Scientists on the scene could only comment that people did not make the lights.

## SHARE THE WEALTH

Marfa is the most famous location for "ghost lights" and "mystery lights," but it's not the only place to see them. Here are just a few of the legendary unexplained lights that attract visitors to dark roads in Texas on murky nights.

• In southeast Texas, a single orb appears regularly near Saratoga on Bragg Road.

• The Anson Light appears near Mt. Hope Cemetery in Anson, by U.S. Highway 180.

• Since 1850, "Brit Bailey's Light" glows five miles west of Angleton near Highway 35 in Brazoria County.

• In January 2008, Stephenville attracted international attention when unexplained lights—and perhaps a metallic spaceship—flew fast and low over the town.

The Marfa Lights appear over Mitchell Flat, which is entirely private property. However, the curious can view the lights from a Texas Highway Department roadside parking area about nine miles east of Marfa on U.S. Highway 90. Seekers should arrive before dusk for the best location, especially during bluebonnet season (mid-April through late May), because this is a popular tourist stop.

The Marfa Lights Festival takes place during Labor Day weekend each year. This annual celebration of Marfa's mystery includes a parade, arts and crafts booths, great food, and a street dance.

# THE BIRTH OF FLYING SAUCERS

Since flying saucers exploded into the public consciousness more than 60 years ago, they have inspired books and films, late night conversations, and congressional hearings. People all over the world have spent countless hours in attempts to unravel the mystery behind them and the variety of phenomena that seem to be related to them. Researchers have turned up reports of strange things in the sky going back millennia, and they continue to today—but it was the story of what happened over the course of two and a half minutes on a Tuesday afternoon in 1947 that brought it all to the world's attention.

It was the afternoon of June 24, a bright, clear day in southern Washington. An Idaho-based businessman named Kenneth Arnold was flying his two-seater airplane east from Chehalis to Yakima. He had taken a little bit of a detour toward Mount Rainier; a Marine C-46 transport plane had crashed in the mountains and the air force was offering a $5,000 reward for the location of the wreckage. Arnold had been involved in search and rescue operations before, and the reward money didn't hurt either.

Right before 3:00 P.M., a flash of light dazzled him. Arnold looked out his windows to see what could have caused it. At first, he thought he was alone except for the DC-4 transport plane that he noticed behind and to his left. Then, thirty seconds later, he saw them: nine objects to the north, flying very fast and in formation from Mount Baker to Mount Rainier. He kept a level head and timed how long it took them to cross the distance between the peaks so he could estimate their speed later. It took them one minute and forty-two seconds. Ducking and weaving around the peaks of the mountain range, they headed on their southward course, flashing in the sun like fish jumping out of the water. Eight of them were roughly circular with metallic mirror-finishes, but the ninth, which was crescent-shaped, was darker. None of them seemed to have any kind of tail section. Whatever they were, they weren't conventional aircraft. Judging their size against the DC-4 behind him, he estimated each of them as being about 60 feet wide, a little under half the wingspan of the cargo plane. Arnold would later compare the graceful way they moved to stones skipped on the water, and their swaying formation to "the tail of a Chinese kite."

The sighting was over quickly: the objects sped on their way and disappeared south beyond Mount Adams. Arnold had seen them for a total of about two and a half minutes. He continued on his way to Yakima, and then headed onward to his final destination of Pendleton, Oregon. A crowd was waiting for him: unbeknownst to Arnold, someone at Yakima had called Pendleton and mentioned the encounter. An airshow was going on, so the field was already full of people who were interested in hearing about what people assumed at first must have been some kind of cutting-edge military hardware.

It was at Pendleton that he realized just how strange this encounter that had given him an "eerie feeling" had been. When he calculated the speed of the objects, he came up with an unbelievable figure: 1,700 miles per hour, more than twice the speed of sound. The *P-80 Shooting Star*, the air force's premier jet fighter at the time, had a top speed under ideal conditions of about 600 miles per hour. Chuck Yeager's famous (and initially very secret) sound barrier-breaking test flight was still months away. Even when he allowed for possible errors in observation, he came away with a figure of 1,200 miles per hour, still faster than any human craft had ever flown. Some people there were reminded of wartime reports of "foo fighters" and other odd things seen in the sky. Despite all that, the general consensus among the pilots was that they had probably been some kind of guided missile or aircraft from the nearby Moses Lake Air Field, where the B-47 and B-50 bombers had been tested during World War II. Some suggested that perhaps the Soviets were somehow involved. Arnold was still unsure.

The next day, after encountering a man from Ukiah who claimed to have also seen "mystery missiles" on the 24th, Kenneth Arnold went to the press. He impressed the reporter with his seriousness and sobriety, and the story was picked up by the Associated Press and quickly spread across the nation. It became apparent that Arnold was not the only person who had seen something strange that day: although details varied, eighteen reports of strange flying objects in the skies above the Pacific Northwest on June 24 eventually came to light. And soon the phenomenon had a name: flying saucers. The first known use of the phrase—apparently inspired by the vivid image Arnold had provided of the objects' motion being like "saucers skipped on water" even more than the roughly circular shape of eight of the nine objects—was in *Chicago Sun* newspaper. Although this-worldly explanations predominated at first, the unprecedented speeds and uncanny nature of the whole affair ensured that speculation about visitors from another world began quickly.

Sightings came in from across the country, some made by airline pilots, police officers, former military officers, and other proverbially trustworthy witnesses. That 4th of July saw an outpouring of reports. And although the story would be quickly retracted and forgotten about for years, a press release came from an air force officer in New Mexico claiming that debris from one of these craft had been recovered.

The age of flying saucers had begun.

## KENNETH ARNOLD

At the time of his famous sighting, Kenneth Arnold was selling and installing fire suppression systems for Great Western Fire Control Supply. Although based in Idaho, his work frequently brought all over the northwestern United States. He was a skilled civilian pilot with many hours of flight time.

After his experience, Arnold spent some time investigating

reports of flying saucers himself, including the convoluted events that took place at Maury Island, and the story of one of the earliest (and most obscure) of the so-called contactees, Samuel Eaton Thompson. Arnold wrote several magazine articles on the phenomenon and eventually a book, *The Coming of the Saucers.*

# ILLUMINATI AND THE NEW WORLD ORDER

The name "Illuminati" has been given to several groups, both real and fictional. University professor Adam Weishaupt founded the "Illuminati" in the Electorate of Bavaria on May 1, 1776. Like many religious faiths and secret societies, the original Bavarian Illuminati were founded in search of enlightenment. Their goals were to support rationalism, secularism, and liberalism, and to oppose superstition, obscurantism, religious influence over public life, and abuses of state power. Bavarian ruler Charles Theodore banned the Illuminati and other secret societies in the 1780s. The Illuminati did not long survive their suppression in Bavaria.

Some conspiracy theorists believe that the Illuminati have survived to this day and are involved in an international conspiracy to create a New World Order. The common theme in conspiracy theories about a New World Order is that a secretive group of elites controls governments, industry, and media organizations, with the goal of establishing world domination.

# FREEMASONS

Conspiracy theorists delight in telling how the Freemasons rose from the ashes of the Knights Templar (an earlier secret society that protected Christians on the road to Jerusalem and supposedly guarded the location of the Holy Grail), founded the United States of America, and continue to shape world politics under the guise of their sister organization, the Illuminati. Conspiracy theories have alleged the Freemasons were involved the 9/11 attacks, faking the

Apollo moon landings, and the murder of President John F. Kennedy. The truth, however, is much more sedate and much less "Hollywood."

Freemasonry is a fraternal organization, originally comprised of stonemasons and craftsmen. Organized Freemasonry emerged in Great Britain in the mid-17th century with the firm establishment of Grand Lodges and smaller, local Lodges. In 1730, transplanted Englishmen established the first American Lodge in Virginia, followed in 1733 by the continent's first chartered and opened Grand Lodge in Massachusetts. Boasting early American members including George Washington, Benjamin Franklin, and John Hancock, Freemasonry played a part in the growth of the young nation in ways that gradually attracted curiosity, speculation, and concern.

The source of the organization's mysterious reputation lay partly in its secrecy: Masons were prohibited from revealing secrets (some believed Masons would be violently punished if they revealed secrets, though the Masons deny such rumors). The Masonic bond also emphasized a commitment to one another. Outsiders feared the exclusivity smacked of conspiracy and compromised the motives of Masons appointed to juries or elected to public office. And nonmembers wondered about the meanings of the Freemasons' peculiar traditions (such as code words and other secretive forms of recognition between members) and symbolism (often geometric shapes or tools, such as the square and compass). Design elements of the one-dollar bill, including the Great Seal and the "all-seeing eye," have been credited to founding fathers such as Charles Thomson and other Masons.

Freemasonry in the United States suffered a serious blow in September 1826 when New York Masons abducted a former "brother" named William Morgan. Morgan was about to publish a book of Masonic secrets, but before he could, he was instead ushered north to the Canadian border and, in all likelihood, thrown into the Niagara River. His disappearance led to the arrest and conviction of three men on kidnapping charges (Morgan's body was never found)— scant penalties, locals said, for crimes that surely included murder. The affair increased widespread suspicion of the brotherhood, spawning an American Anti-Mason movement and even a new political party dedicated to keeping Freemasons out of national office.

In the decades following the Civil War, men were again drawn to brotherhood and fellowship as they searched for answers in a changing age, and Freemasonry slowly regained popularity.

# ONE REPTILE TO RULE THEM ALL

Some people are ruled by their pets; others are ruled by their work. Conspiracy theorist David Icke believes that we're all being ruled by reptilian humanoids.

## WORLDWIDE DOMINATION

David Icke has worn many hats: journalist, news anchor for the BBC, spokesman for the British Green Party, and professional soccer player. But after a spiritual experience in Peru in 1991, he took on another role: famed conspiracy theorist.

Like many other conspiracy theorists, Icke believes that a group called the Illuminati, or "global elite," controls the world. According to these theorists, the group manipulates the economy and uses mind control to usher humanity into a submissive state. Icke also believes that the group is responsible for organizing such tragedies as the Holocaust and the Oklahoma City bombings.

Some of the most powerful people in the world are members, claims Icke, including ex-British Prime Minister Tony Blair and former U.S. President George H. W. Bush, as well as leaders of financial institutions and major media outlets. However, not all members are human. According to Icke, those at the top of the Illuminati bloodlines are vehicles for a reptilian entity from the constellation Draco. These shape-shifters can change from human to reptile and back again, and they are essentially controlling humanity.

## IS ICKE ONTO SOMETHING?

In the documentary *David Icke: Was He Right?*, Icke claims that many of his earlier predictions, including a hurricane in New Orleans and a "major attack on a large city" between the years 2000 and 2002, have come true. But are we really being ruled by reptilian humanoids or is Icke's theory a bunch of snake oil? Icke was nearly laughed off the stage in a 1991 appearance on a BBC talk show. But with 16 published books, thousands attending his speaking engagements, and nearly 200,000 weekly hits to his Web site, perhaps it's Icke who's having the last laugh.

# SCANDALOUS CULTS

## BRANCH DAVIDIANS

Followers of David Koresh looked upon him as one of God's messengers. Koresh thought of himself the same way. The U.S. government, however, had a different point of view (including allegations of polygamy, child abuse, and rape). Koresh and many followers of his religious sect were killed in 1993 when federal agents attempted to raid the group's compound near Waco, Texas. The ensuing 51-day standoff ended on April 19 when the Branch Davidian compound burned to the ground. The fallout wasn't limited to Koresh and company—the federal government was highly criticized for its handling of the situation.

## HEAVEN'S GATE

UFOs and Comet Hale-Bopp were the basis of this cult, which was led by Marshall Applewhite. Members believed that Earth was about to be "recycled" and instead opted to commit mass suicide. Thirty-nine members of the cult (including Applewhite as well as the brother of *Star Trek* actress Nichelle Nichols) were found dead in a San Diego mansion in 1997.

## MANSON FAMILY

More than 40 years after his followers murdered Leno and Rosemary LaBianca and actress Sharon Tate, the name "Charles Manson" still sends a chill down the spines of many people. Manson was charged with murder and conspiracy and served a life sentence until his death in 2017. Among the members of the Manson family was Lynette "Squeaky" Fromme, who attempted to assassinate President Gerald R. Ford in 1975.

## THE PEOPLE'S TEMPLE

About 900 followers of a quasi-religious group led by Reverend Jim Jones drank cyanide as part of a mass suicide in Jonestown, Guyana, in 1978. Many experts view the event as one of the largest mass suicides in recorded history. For the record, Jones chose not to imbibe of the poisonous drink he offered the others. He shot himself in the head instead. Oh, but the story isn't over. Before things fell apart at his headquarters, Jones ordered a group of his followers to a nearby Georgetown airstrip to stop the departure of some People's Temple followers who had lost the faith. The armed men opened fire on the group as they were departing. Among those killed was U.S. Representative Leo Ryan of California, who had traveled to Guyana to investigate the cult on the behalf of concerned family members.

# THE KNIGHTS OF THE GOLDEN CIRCLE

Though documentation proves this secret organization to preserve the Southern cause did indeed exist, many mysteries remain about the Knights of the Golden Circle.

The Knights of the Golden Circle was a pro-South organization that operated out of the Deep South, the border states, the Midwest, and even parts of the North both before and during the Civil War. Much of its history is unknown due to its underground nature, but it is known that this secret society, bound by passwords, rituals, and handshakes, intended to preserve Southern culture and states' rights. Its precise origin, membership, and purpose are documented in a handful of primary sources, including the club's handbook, an exposé published in 1861, and a wartime government report that revealed the K.G.C. to be a serious threat to the federal government and its effort to quash the rebellion and maintain the Union.

Some historians trace the organization of the Knights of the Golden Circle back to the 1830s, though the name did not surface publicly until 1855. According to a report by the U.S. government in 1864, the organization included as many as 500,000 members in the North alone and had "castles," or local chapters, spread across the country. Members included everyone from notable politicians to the rank and file, all prepared to rise up against federal coercion as they saw their rights to slavery slipping away.

## WHAT'S IN A NAME?

The group's name referred to a geographic "Golden Circle" that surrounded the Deep South. Its boundaries were the border states on the north, America's western territories, Mexico, Central America, and even Cuba. Southern leaders and organization members hoped to gain control of these lands to create a strong, agrarian economy dependent on slavery and plantations. This would either balance the numbers of slave states to free states in the federal government or provide a distinct nation that could separate from the Union. The proslavery leader John C. Calhoun of South Carolina was the group's intellectual mentor, although the K.G.C. didn't likely achieve great numbers before his death in 1850. The 1864 government report cited that members initially used nuohlac, Calhoun spelled backward, as a password.

## ADDING FUEL TO THE FIRE

Once the Civil War began, the K.G.C. became a concern for both state and federal governments. The most obvious public figure associated with the K.G.C. was Dr. George Bickley, an eccentric pamphleteer of questionable character. He is credited with organizing the first castle of the Knights of the Golden Circle in his hometown of Cincinnati. He also sent an open letter to the Kentucky legislature declaring that his organization had 8,000 members in the state, with representatives in every county. The legislature called for a committee to investigate the organization, which had begun to menace that state's effort to remain neutral by importing arms and ammunition for the secession cause. Federal officers arrested Bickley in New Albany, Indiana, in 1863 with a copy of the society's Rules, Regulations, and Principles of the K.G.C. and other regalia on his person. He was held in the Ohio state prison until late 1865. Bickley died two years later, never having been formally charged with a crime.

## METHODS AND TACTICS

The underground group used subversive tactics to thwart the Lincoln administration's effort once the war began. A telegram between a Union colonel and Secretary of War Edwin Stanton states how the "Holy Brotherhood" sought to encourage Union soldiers to desert and to paint the conflict as a war in favor of abolition. Some of the government's more questionable wartime tactics, such as the suspension of habeas corpus and the quelling of some aspects of a free press, were rallying points in the Midwest, and they were issues that surely connected northern dissidents such as Copperheads with the Knights in spirit if not in reality. When antiwar sentiment and Peace Democrats influenced populations in Indiana, a U.S. court subpoenaed witnesses for a grand jury to learn more about the organization. The grand jury claimed the secret organization had recruited 15,000 members in Indiana alone and indicted 60 people in August 1862. The Union army attempted to infiltrate the organization and expose its subversive operations by sending new recruits back home to join the K.G.C.

## POLITICAL TIES

Nationally known political leaders were also allegedly tied to the group. The 1861 exposé referred to a certain "Mr. V—of Ohio" as one of the few reliable members among prominent Northern politicians. It would likely have been assumed that this referred to leading Copperhead and Ohio Representative Clement Vallandigham, who decried abolition before the war and criticized Republicans in Congress and the administration. Union officers arrested Vallandigham, and a military court exiled him to the South. Another possible member was John C. Breckenridge, vice president under James Buchanan and a presidential candidate in 1860. Even former President Franklin Pierce was accused of having an affiliation with the organization.

## ASSASSINATION CONSPIRACY

Some also believe that the K.G.C. had a hand in the assassination of Abraham Lincoln. The contemporary exposé stated, "Some one of them is to distinguish himself for—if he can, that is—the assassination of the 'Abolition' President." According to a later anonymous account, Lincoln's assassin, John Wilkes Booth, took the oath of the society in a Baltimore castle in the fall of 1860.

The organization had several counterparts during the war, including the Knights of the Golden Square, the Union Relief Society, the Order of American Knights, and the Order of the Sons of Liberty, to name a few.

# THE HOUSE OF DAVID

The only thing more startling than seeing men with waist-length hair and long beards playing baseball in the early

1900s might have been knowing every player on this early barnstorming team was a member of a highly controversial religious sect known as the House of David.

## FROM KENTUCKY TO THE SECOND COMING

Based in Benton Harbor, Michigan, this religious sect centered on its charismatic leader, Benjamin Franklin Purnell, and his wife, Mary. The couple believed that they were God's appointed messengers for the Second Coming of Christ, and that the human body could have eternal life on Earth. They also believed that both men and women should imitate Jesus by never cutting their hair. Purnell based his teachings on those of an 18th-century English group called the Philadelphians, which were developed from the prophecies of a woman named Joanna Southcott who claimed she was the first of seven messengers to proclaim the Second Coming. Purnell somehow deduced that he was also one of those seven.

## GROWING HAIR, RELIGION, AND CROWDS

Born in Kentucky in March 1861, Purnell and his wife Mary traveled around the country for several years while polishing their doctrine. After being booted out of a small town in Ohio, possibly because Benjamin was accused of adultery with a local farmer's wife, they landed in Benton Harbor in March 1903. Members of a sect related to the Philadelphians called the Jezreelites lived in nearby Grand Rapids, and Purnell had been in touch with the Bauschke brothers of Benton Harbor, who were sympathetic to his cause.

With the backing of the Bauschkes and other prominent local citizens, Purnell soon attracted a crowd of believers and called his group the Israelite House of David. The

700 or so members lived chaste, commune-style lives on a cluster of farms and land, served vegetarian meals, and started successful cottage industries, such as a toy factory, greenhouse, and canning facility.

As word spread of the longhaired, oddly dressed members and their colony, the curious began making Sunday trips to observe them. Purnell turned this into a cash opportunity by opening an aviary, a small zoo, a vegetarian restaurant, an ice-cream parlor, and, ironically, a barber shop. The crowds grew, and, in 1908, he started work on his own amusement park, which included an expanded zoo and a miniature, steam-powered railway whose trains ran throughout the grounds.

## ENTERTAINMENT EVANGELISM

In the meantime, some members of the group had formed a baseball team that also drew crowds, so Purnell added a large stadium next to the amusement park. The team traveled as well, and added to their popularity with comical routines, such as hiding the ball under their beards. Building on the sports theme, the colony also featured exhibition basketball, and later, miniature car racing.

The colony also boasted a popular brass band, whose members capitalized on their showy long tresses by starting each concert facing away from the audience, hair covering half of their snazzy uniforms. They often played jazzy, crowd-pleasing numbers rather than the expected somber religious tunes.

Religious activities continued, too. Adopting the title "The Prince of Peace," Purnell often held teaching sessions, including one in which he was photographed allegedly changing water into wine.

## PROBLEMS IN PARADISE

As happens with any large social enterprise, some members became disgruntled and left. Purnell referred to them as "scorpions." Rumors flew concerning improper relations between Purnell and young females in the group, especially when the colony purchased an island in northern Michigan where they ran a prosperous lumber business. Newspaper reports alleged that rebellious group members were killed and buried there and that Purnell kept a group of young girls as sex slaves. The public was also suspicious of mass weddings he conducted. Lawsuits had begun against Purnell in Ohio and continued to mount even as the Michigan colony progressed.

In 1926, Purnell was finally arrested on charges that included religious fraud and statutory rape. He endured a lengthy trial, but he was ill for most of it, and much of his testimony was deemed incoherent. Most charges were eventually dismissed.

Purnell died in Benton Harbor on December 16, 1927, at age 66. But shortly before passing, he told his followers that, like Jesus, he would be back in three days. As far as anyone knows, he wasn't. His preserved remains were kept in a glass-covered coffin on the colony grounds for decades, although at one time Mary's brother reportedly insisted that the body was not Purnell's but that of another colony member.

## REMAINS OF THE DAY

After his death, some of the believers switched their allegiance to Purnell's widow, Mary, who lived until 1953 and started a new colony called Mary's City of David, which still plays baseball and runs a museum in Benton Harbor. The grounds and businesses were split between the two groups, and only a handful of members remain in either. The zoo closed in 1945, with the animals given to Chicago's Lincoln Park Zoo, and the amusement park, remembered fondly by many local residents, closed in the early 1970s. The original area east of Benton Harbor's city limits still serves as the headquarters for the two groups. And many credit Benjamin Purnell as the forerunner of later, high-style evangelical leaders such as Jim Bakker and Oral Roberts.

The House of David team played in the first professional night baseball game, in Independence, Kansas, in 1930.

# THE INTERGALACTIC JOURNEY OF SCIENTOLOGY

There are few who don't know about the aura of mystery and scandal that surrounds the Church of Scientology, which boasts a small membership and a seismic pocketbook. Scientology frequently graces the headlines with stories ranging from accounts of Tom Cruise tomfoolery to an endless stream of lawsuits and accusations of bribery and abuse.

The fantastical elements to the saga of Scientology were perhaps written into the religion from its beginning, given that Scientology sprang from the fertile mind of its late creator, pulp fiction writer turned religious messiah, L. Ron Hubbard. Hubbard, born in 1911, began his writing career in the 1930s after flunking out of college. Hubbard had always preferred imagination to reality: Accounts of his past reveal hallucinogenic drug abuse and an obsession with black magic and Satanism. In between prolific bouts of writing, Hubbard served in the Navy during World War II, became involved in various start-up ventures, and, of course, dabbled in black magic ceremonies. Allegation has it that Hubbard and wealthy scientist friend John Parsons performed a ritual in which they attempted to impregnate a woman with the antichrist. The woman was Parsons's girlfriend, but she soon became Hubbard's second wife—though he was still married to his first wife.

## DOWN TO A SCIENCE

In 1949, Hubbard developed a self-help process that he called Dianetics. All of humanity's problems, according to Dianetics, stem from the traumas of past lives. These traumas are called engrams, and Hubbard's own e-meter (a machine using simple lie detector technology) can identify and help eliminate these engrams. Getting rid of engrams can have amazing results—from increasing intelligence to curing blindness. The first Dianetics article appeared in a sci-fi publication called *Astounding Science Fiction*. In 1950, Hubbard opened the Hubbard Dianetic Research Foundation in New Jersey, and in that same year *Dianetics: The Modern Science of Mental Health* was published and sold well.

Hubbard and his followers attempted to establish Dianetics as an official science. But the medical profession didn't appreciate Dianetics masquerading as science. The Dianetic Research Foundation came under investigation by the IRS and the American Medical Association. Hubbard closed his clinics and fled New Jersey.

## ACTUALLY, IT'S A RELIGION...

Dianetics wasn't making the cut as a scientific theory, so Hubbard played another card. Years before, Hubbard is reputed to have told a friend "writing for a penny a word is ridiculous. If a man really wants to make a million dollars, the best way would be to start his own religion." After fleeing Jersey, Hubbard moved to Phoenix, Arizona, declared Dianetics an "applied religious philosophy," and, in 1954, Hubbard's organization was recognized as a religion by the IRS and granted tax-exempt status.

Thus the Church of Scientology was born. Hubbard added new stories to the original Dianetics creation, and by the 1960s, humans were spiritual descendants of the alien Thetans, who were banished to live on Earth by the intergalactic terrorist dictator Xenu 75 million years ago. Scientologist disciples must not only expel the traumas of past lives but of past lives on different planets. Discovering these traumas is an expensive process, so the Church actively recruits wealthy devotees. As for Hubbard, he died in 1986, soon after the IRS accused him of stealing $200 million from the Church. Today, Scientology and its various offshoot nonprofit groups and private business ventures continue to hold a vast fortune, and Scientology's ongoing litigation with the IRS, the press, and ex-devotees (hundreds of lawsuits are pending) are so bizarre, they seem almost out of this world.

# UNBELIEVABLE BELIEFS

## THE HOLLOW EARTH THEORY

In the early 19th century, John Cleves Symmes promoted the Hollow Earth Theory, which stated that the planet was actually several populated worlds nesting inside one another. Symmes's ideas influenced Cyrus Teed, who developed Koreshan Unity, a religion based on the theory. For about 100 years, Koreshan Unity drew thousands of followers worldwide. The Hollow Earth Theory was revived during World War II, when some authors theorized that the Nazis actually came from an underground civilization. More recently, Kevin and Matthew Taylor spent 12 years investigating the idea; they wrote a book about their findings, *The Land of No Horizon.*

## THE MILLERITES

William Miller, a farmer in northern New York, founded a doomsday cult in the 1800s. Studying the Bible convinced Miller that humanity was due for damnation. He began preaching this message in the early 1830s. His first prediction was that Jesus Christ would "come again to the earth, cleanse, purify and take possession of the same" between March 1843 and March 1844. When a comet appeared early in 1843, a number of his followers killed themselves, believing the end was near. However, when his prophecy didn't come to pass and the world survived, Miller stood by his message but became reluctant to set actual dates. Some of his followers took it upon themselves to announce October 22, 1844, as the big day, and Miller reluctantly agreed. This date came to be known as The Great Disappointment. Regardless, Miller and his followers established a basis on which the Seventh-Day Adventist Church was later founded.

## THE VAMPIRE CHURCH

With offices located throughout the United States, Canada, and Australia, the Vampire Church provides the initiated and the curious with an opportunity to learn more about vampirism. However, don't expect to find much about the "undead," as vampires have been portrayed in stories since Bram Stoker wrote *Dracula* in 1897. Instead, the church offers insight into vampirism as a physical condition that sometimes requires unusual energy resources, such as blood. In addition, it explains the difference between psychic vampires and elemental vampires. According to the church's Web site, "The Vampire Church continues to grow as more true vampires find the haven they so seek with others of this condition and the knowledge and experience of others here."

## THE CHURCH OF EUTHANASIA

"Save the Planet—Kill Yourself." These words are the battle cry of the Church of Euthanasia, which was established by Boston resident Chris Korda in 1992. Korda, a musician, had a dream one night about an alien who warned her that Earth was in serious danger. The extraterrestrial, which Korda dubbed "The Being," stressed the importance of protecting the planet's environment through population control. As a result of the encounter, Korda established the Church of Euthanasia, which supports suicide, abortion, and sodomy (defined as any sex act that is not intended for procreation). According to the church's Web site, members are vegetarian, but they "support cannibalism for those who insist on eating flesh." Although it reportedly has only about 100 members in the Boston area, the church claims that thousands worldwide have visited its Web site and been exposed to its message.

## SNAKE-HANDLING PENTECOSTAL SECTS

In describing the casting out of devils, the speaking in tongues, and the healing of the sick by the laying on of hands, Mark 16:17–18 is a veritable mother lode of guidelines for fundamentalist Christian sects throughout America. But it is another claim of those verses that has led to perhaps the most bizarre and dangerous of the Christian

sects: the admonition that followers "shall take up serpents."
These four words, considered symbolic by most Christian
scholars, are considered the literal command of God by a
small number of snake-handling Pentecostal sects, mostly
located in the rural Appalachia region of the southeastern
United States. Snake-handling rituals have been around
for the better part of a century, and they show no signs of
disappearing. According to Pentecostal leaders, handling
poisonous snakes is ordained by scripture, and practitioners
are fully aware of the dangers involved. There have been
more than 100 fatalities attributed to the practice, with
thousands more injured.

# 9/11 CONSPIRACY THEORIES

September 11, 2001, will live in infamy as the nation's worst
terrorist attack. Islamic extremists hijacked four commercial
airliners, crashing two of the planes into the North and South
towers of the World Trade Center in New York City, and a
third plane into the Pentagon. A fourth airliner crashed into a
field in rural Pennsylvania as passengers attempted to regain
control of the aircraft from the hijackers. The 9/11 attacks
killed nearly 3,000 people, injured more than 6,000, and
launched an American-led war on terrorism. The attacks also
provoked a wide variety of conspiracy theories. Proponents
of these theories dispute some or all of the facts in the
official version of the story told to the public.

## CONTROLLED DEMOLITION THEORIES

One of the most prominent 9/11 conspiracy theories is that
the collapse of both World Trade Center towers resulted
from controlled demolitions using explosives planted prior
to 9/11.

## THEORY:

Controlled demolition theorists claim that the aircraft impacts
and subsequent fires could not have weakened the buildings
sufficiently to cause their collapse. They argue that jet fuel
from the aircraft could not burn hot enough to melt steel.
Proponents also point to clouds of dust seen blowing out of
windows as evidence of explosive charges.

## FACT:

The National Institute of Standards and Technology (NIST) and the magazine *Popular Mechanics*, among others, examined and rejected these theories. The NIST investigation "found no corroborating evidence for alternative hypotheses suggesting that the WTC towers were brought down by controlled demolition using explosives planted prior to Sept. 11, 2001." While the jet fuel did not melt the buildings' steel structures, it significantly weakened them. And experts identify the clouds of dust seen blowing out of the windows as air—along with pulverized concrete, paper, and other debris—being forced out of windows as floors collapsed on each other, not evidence of explosives.

Based on its comprehensive investigation, NIST concluded that the WTC towers collapsed because: "(1) the impact of the planes severed and damaged support columns, dislodged fireproofing insulation coating the steel floor trusses and steel columns, and widely dispersed jet fuel over multiple floors; and (2) the subsequent unusually large jet-fuel ignited multi-floor fires (which reached temperatures as high as 1,000 degrees Celsius) significantly weakened the floors and columns with dislodged fireproofing to the point where floors sagged and pulled inward on the perimeter columns. This led to the inward bowing of the perimeter columns and failure of the south face of WTC 1 and the east face of WTC 2, initiating the collapse of each of the towers."

## THE PENTAGON ATTACK

Another prominent 9/11 conspiracy theory is that a missile, not American Airlines flight 77, hit the Pentagon.

### THEORY:

Conspiracy theorists claim that the two holes punched into the side of the Pentagon were much smaller than the wingspan of a 757.

### FACT:

Investigators concluded that the main hole in the Pentagon's exterior wall, Ring E, was smaller than the plane's wingspan because one wing hit the ground and the other was sheared off on impact. The second, smaller hole in Ring C was made by the jet's landing gear.

Here are some other facts conspiracy theorists tend to dismiss or ignore:

• The remains of American Airlines flight 77 crew and passengers were found at the Pentagon crash site, and positively identified by DNA.

• Dozens of eyewitnesses saw the plane strike the Pentagon. Some saw passengers through the plane's windows.

• Photographs and eyewitness reports show plane debris at the Pentagon crash site, as was also witnessed by survivors and rescue personnel.

• The flight's black boxes were also recovered at the site.

• Phone calls from passengers on American Airlines flight 77 reported that it had been hijacked.

• High-ranking Al Qaeda members acknowledged that they carried out the 9/11 attacks.

## STAND DOWN ORDER

### THEORY:

None of the fighter jets from any of the 28 air force bases within range of the hijacked planes were scrambled because they had been ordered to stand down.

### FACT:

The Federal Aviation Administration's Boston Center called the Northeast Air Defense Sector (NEADS) at 8:37 A.M. to inform them that American Airlines flight 11 was hijacked. Within minutes, NEADS scrambled two F-15s from Otis Air National Guard Base at Falmouth, Massachusetts, and three F-16s from Langley Air National Guard Base in Hampton, Virginia. The 9/11 Commission Report stated, "Planes were scrambled, but ineffectively, as they did not know where to go or what targets they were to intercept."

Additionally, when the hijackers turned off the planes' transponders, Air Traffic Control had to look through thousands of radar blips to find the planes. The North American Aerospace Defense Command (NORAD) had its radar focused on threats coming from outside the country rather than internal attacks. As the 9/11 Commission Report stated, "America's homeland defenders faced outward."

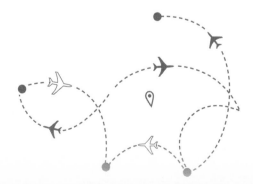

# FOREKNOWLEDGE

One of the most common 9/11 conspiracy theories is that the U.S. government had advance knowledge of the attacks and either deliberately ignored or assisted the attackers.

## THEORY:

Insider trading in United Airlines and American Airlines stocks just before September 11, 2001, is evidence of advance knowledge of the plot. Allegations of insider trading in advance of September 11 generally rest on reports of unusual pre-9/11 trading activity in companies whose stock plummeted after the attacks.

## FACT:

The bipartisan 9/11 Commission investigated the issue and concluded, "Some unusual trading did in fact occur, but each such trade proved to have an innocuous explanation." For example, the Commission stated in its final report, "much of the seemingly suspicious trading in American on September 10 was traced to a specific U.S.-based options trading newsletter, faxed to its subscribers on Sunday, September 9, which recommended these trades."

# THE MEN ON THE MOON

On July 20, 1969, millions of people worldwide watched in awe as U.S. astronauts became the first humans to step on the moon. However, a considerable number of conspiracy theorists contend that the men were just actors performing on a soundstage.

The National Aeronautics and Space Administration (NASA) has been dealing with this myth for over 40 years. In fact, it has a page on its official Web site that scientifically explains the pieces of "proof" that supposedly expose the fraud. These are the most common questions raised.

If the astronauts really did take photographs on the moon, why aren't the stars visible in them? The stars are there but are too faint to be seen in the photos. The reason for this has to do with the fact that the lunar surface is so brightly lit by the sun. The astronauts had to adjust their camera settings to accommodate the brightness, which then rendered the stars in the background difficult to see.

Why was there no blast crater under the lunar module? The astronauts had slowed their descent, bringing the rocket on the lander from a maximum of 10,000 pounds of thrust to just 3,000 pounds. In addition, the lack of atmosphere on the moon spread the exhaust fairly wide, lowering the pressure and diminishing the scope of a blast crater.

If there is no air on the moon, why does the flag planted by the astronauts appear to be waving? The flag appears to wave because the astronauts were rotating the pole on which it was mounted as they tried to get it to stand upright.

When the lunar module took off from the moon back into orbit, why was there no visible flame from the rocket? The composition of the fuel used for the takeoff from the surface of the moon was different in that it produced no flame.

Conspiracy theorists present dozens of "examples" that supposedly prove that the moon landing never happened, and all of them are easily explained. But that hasn't kept naysayers from perpetuating the myth.

Twenty-three years after the moon landing, on February 15, 2001, Fox TV stirred the pot yet again with a program titled *Conspiracy Theory: Did We Land on the Moon?* The show trotted out the usual array of conspiracy theorists who in turn dusted off the usual spurious "proof." And once again, NASA found itself having to answer to a skeptical but persistent few.

Many people theorize that the landing was faked because the United States didn't have the technology to safely send a crew to the moon. Instead, it pretended it did as a way to win the final leg of the space race against the Soviet Union. But consider the situation: Thousands of men and women worked for almost a decade (and three astronauts died) to make the success of *Apollo 11* a reality. With so many people involved, a hoax of that magnitude would be virtually impossible to contain, especially after four decades.

For additional proof that the moon landing really happened, consider the hundreds of pounds of moon rocks brought back by the six *Apollo* missions that were able to retrieve them. Moon rocks are unique and aren't easily manufactured, so if they didn't come from the moon, what is their source? Finally, there's no denying the fact that the *Apollo* astronauts left behind a two-foot reflecting panel equipped with dozens of tiny mirrors. Scientists are able to bounce laser pulses off the mirrors to pinpoint the moon's distance from Earth.

The myth of the faked moon landing will probably never go

away. But the proof of its reality is irrefutable. In the words of astronaut Charles Duke, who walked on the moon in 1972 as part of the *Apollo 16* mission: "We've been to the moon nine times. Why would we fake it nine times, if we faked it?"

# THE PHILADELPHIA EXPERIMENT

In 1943, the navy destroyer USS *Eldridge* reportedly vanished, teleported from a dock in Pennsylvania to one in Virginia, and then rematerialized—all as part of a top-secret military experiment. Is there any fact to this fiction?

## THE GENESIS OF A MYTH

The story of the Philadelphia Experiment began with the scribbled annotations of a crazed genius, Carlos Allende, who in 1956 read *The Case for the UFO*, by science enthusiast Morris K. Jessup. Allende wrote chaotic annotations in his copy of the book, claiming, among other things, to know the answers to all the scientific and mathematical questions that Jessup's book touched upon. Jessup's interests included the possible military applications of electromagnetism, antigravity, and Einstein's Unified Field Theory.

Allende wrote two letters to Jessup, warning him that the government had already put Einstein's ideas to dangerous use. According to Allende, at some unspecified date in October 1943, he was serving aboard a merchant ship when he witnessed a disturbing naval experiment. The USS *Eldridge* disappeared, teleported from Philadelphia, Pennsylvania, to Norfolk, Virginia, and then reappeared in a matter of minutes. The men onboard the ship allegedly phased in and out of visibility or lost their minds and jumped overboard, and a few of them disappeared forever. This strange activity was part of an apparently successful military experiment to render ships invisible.

## THE NAVY GETS INVOLVED

Allende could not provide Jessup with any evidence for these claims, so Jessup stopped the correspondence. But in 1956, Jessup was summoned to Washington, D.C., by the Office of Naval Research, which had received Allende's annotated copy of Jessup's book and wanted to know about Allende's claims and his written comments. Shortly thereafter, Varo Corporation, a private group that does research for the military, published the annotated book, along with the letters Allende had sent to Jessup. The navy has consistently denied Allende's claims about teleporting ships, and the impetus for publishing Allende's annotations is unclear. Morris Jessup committed suicide in 1959, leading some conspiracy theorists to claim that the government had him murdered for knowing too much about the experiments.

## THE FACT WITHIN THE FICTION

It is not certain when Allende's story was deemed the "Philadelphia Experiment," but over time, sensationalist books and movies have touted it as such. The date of the ship's disappearance is usually cited as October 28, though Allende himself cannot verify the date nor identify other witnesses. However, the inspiration behind Allende's claims is not a complete mystery.

In 1943, the navy was in fact conducting experiments, some of which were surely top secret, and sometimes they involved research into the applications of some of Einstein's theories. The navy had no idea how to make ships invisible, but it did want to make ships "invisible"—i.e., undetectable—to enemy magnetic torpedoes. Experiments such as these involved wrapping large cables around navy vessels and pumping them with electricity in order to descramble their magnetic signatures.

# OPERATION NORTHWOODS

On March 13, 1962, a set of proposals on Cuba by the Joint Chiefs of Staff (JCS) was presented in document titled "Justification for U.S. Military Intervention in Cuba." Codenamed Operation Northwords, the proposals called for false flag terrorist attacks to be carried out against American civilians and military targets and blamed on the Cuban government of Fidel Castro as a pretext for invading Cuba. The proposals included the possible assassination of Cuban émigrés, sinking boats of Cuban refugees on the high seas, hijacking planes, blowing up a U.S. ship, and orchestrating terrorism in U.S. cities to create public support for war. President John F. Kennedy rejected the proposals.

# TWA FLIGHT 800

A Boeing 747 out of JFK Airport with 230 people aboard blew up south of Long Island on July 17, 1996. There were no survivors and the plane was destroyed by the explosion, breakup, and fire. Numerous conspiracy theories made the rounds, including that the crash was the result of an on-board bomb, a missile strike, or electromagnetic interference emitted from a U.S. military craft. The FBI found no evidence of a criminal act. The National Transportation Safety Board (NTSB) found that the probable cause was an explosion of the center wing fuel tank, resulting from ignition of the flammable fuel/air mixture in the tank, but that it couldn't determine the source of ignition energy for the explosion with certainty.

A 2013 documentary titled *TWA Flight 800* alleged that the crash investigation was a cover-up and included testimony from former investigators who raised doubts about the NTSB's conclusions. Six retired members of the original investigation team filed a petition to reopen the probe in June 2013, but the NTSB denied the petition.

# GULF OF TONKIN INCIDENT

On August 2, 1964, the destroyer USS *Maddox* was performing a signals intelligence patrol in the Gulf of Tonkin when it was pursued by three North Vietnamese Navy torpedo boats. The USS *Maddox* fired three warning shots and the North Vietnamese boats then attacked with torpedoes and machine gun fire. Three North Vietnamese torpedo boats were damaged, four North Vietnamese sailors were killed, and six more were wounded in the incident on August 2. There were no U.S. casualties and the USS *Maddox* was virtually unscathed.

On August 4, 1964, the USS *Maddox* and the destroyer *Turner Joy* were reportedly under attack by North Vietnamese torpedo boats. In a television address to the American public on August 4, President Lyndon B. Johnson said that the initial August 2 attack on the destroyer *Maddox* was repeated on August 4 by a number of hostile vessels attacking two U.S. destroyers with torpedoes and that he had ordered retaliatory military action in reply.

Days later, Congress passed the Gulf of Tonkin Resolution in response to the incident, which granted President Johnson the authority "to take all necessary steps, including the use of armed force, to assist any member or protocol state of the Southeast Asia Collective Defense Treaty requesting assistance in defense of its freedom." The resolution served as Johnson's legal justification for deploying U.S. conventional forces and the commencement of open warfare against North Vietnam.

In October 2005, the *New York Times* reported that Robert J. Hanyok, a National Security Agency historian, concluded that the NSA deliberately distorted signals intelligence (SIGINT) reports passed to policy makers regarding the August 4, 1964, incident. Hanyok argued that the SIGINT confirmed that North Vietnamese torpedo boats attacked the USS *Maddox* on August 2, 1964, although under questionable circumstances. The SIGINT also showed, according to Hanyok, that a second attack, on August 4, 1964, by North Vietnamese torpedo boats on U.S. ships, did not occur despite claims to the contrary by the Johnson administration.

The USS *Maddox* is refueled in the South China Sea in 1964.

# THE REAL MANCHURIAN CANDIDATES

From the mid-1950s through at least the early 1970s, thousands of unwitting Americans and Canadians became part of a bizarre CIA research project codenamed MKULTRA. Participants were secretly "brainwashed"— drugged with LSD and other hallucinogens, subjected to electro-convulsive shock therapy, and manipulated with abusive mind-control techniques.

MKULTRA began in 1953 under the orders of CIA director Allen Dulles. The program, which was in direct violation of the human rights provisions of the Nuremberg Code that the United States helped establish after WWII, was developed in response to reports that U.S. prisoners of war in Korea were being subjected to Communist mind-control techniques.

CIA researchers hoped to find a "truth drug" that could be used on Soviet agents, as well as drugs that could be used against foreign leaders (one documented scheme involved an attempt in 1960 to dose Fidel Castro with LSD). They also aimed to develop means of mind control that would benefit U.S. intelligence, perhaps including the creation of so-called "Manchurian Candidates" to carry out assassinations. As part of MKULTRA, the CIA investigated parapsychology and such phenomena as hypnosis, telepathy, precognition, photokinesis, and "remote viewing."

MKULTRA was headed by Dr. Sidney Gottlieb, a military psychiatrist and chemist known as the "Black Sorcerer," who specialized in concocting deadly poisons. More than 30 universities and scientific institutes took part in MKULTRA. LSD and other mind-altering drugs including heroin, mescaline, psilocybin, scopolamine, marijuana, and sodium pentothal were given to CIA employees, military personnel, and other government workers, often without the subjects' knowledge or prior consent. To broaden their subject pool, researchers targeted unsuspecting civilians, often those in vulnerable or socially compromising situations. Prison inmates, prostitutes, and mentally ill hospital patients were often used. In a project codenamed Operation Midnight Climax, the CIA set up brothels in several U.S. cities to lure men as unwitting test subjects. Rooms were equipped with cameras that filmed the experiments behind one-way mirrors. Some civilian subjects who consented to participation were used for more extreme experimentation. One group of volunteers in Kentucky was given LSD for more than 70 straight days.

In the 1960s, Dr. Gottlieb also traveled to Vietnam and conducted mind-control experiments on Viet Cong prisoners of war being held by U.S. forces. During the same time period, an unknown number of Soviet agents died in U.S. custody in Europe after being given dual intravenous injections of barbiturates and amphetamine in the CIA's search for a truth serum.

MKULTRA experiments were also carried out in Montreal, Canada, between 1957 and 1964 by Dr. Donald Ewen Cameron, a researcher in Albany, New York, who also served as president of the World Psychiatric Association and the American and Canadian psychiatric associations. The CIA appears to have given him potentially deadly experiments to carry out at Canadian mental health institutes so U.S. citizens would not be involved. Cameron also experimented with paralytic drugs—in some cases inducing a coma in subjects for up to three months—as well as using electro-convulsive therapy at 30 times the normal voltage. The subjects were often women being treated for anxiety disorders and postpartum depression. Many suffered permanent damage. A lawsuit by victims of the experiments later uncovered that the Canadian government had also funded the project.

At least one American subject died in the experiments. Frank Olson, a U.S. Army biological weapons researcher, was secretly given LSD in 1953. A week later, he fell from a hotel window in New York City following a severe psychotic episode. A CIA doctor assigned to monitor Olson claimed he jumped from the window, but an autopsy performed on Olson's exhumed remains in 1994 found that he had been knocked unconscious before the fall.

The U.S. Army also conducted experiments with psychoactive drugs. A later investigation determined that nearly all army experiments involved soldiers and civilians who had given their informed consent, and that army researchers had largely followed scientific and safety protocols. Ken Kesey, who would later write *One Flew Over the Cuckoo's Nest* and become one of the originators of the hippie movement, volunteered for LSD studies at an army research center in San Francisco in 1960. LSD stolen from the army lab by test subjects was some of the first in the world used "recreationally" by civilians. The army's high ethical standards, however, seem to have been absent in at least one case. Harold Blauer, a professional tennis player in New York City who was hospitalized for depression following his divorce, died from apparent cardiac arrest during an army experiment in 1952. Blauer had been secretly injected with massive doses of mescaline.

CIA researchers eventually concluded that the effects of LSD were too unpredictable to be useful, and the agency later acknowledged that their experiments made little scientific sense. Records on 150 MKULTRA research projects were destroyed in 1973 by order of CIA Director Richard Helms. A year later, the *New York Times* first reported about CIA experiments on U.S. citizens. In 1975, congressional hearings and a report by the Rockefeller Commission revealed details of the program. In 1976, President Gerald Ford issued an executive order prohibiting experimentation with drugs on human subjects without their informed consent. Ford and CIA Director William Colby also publicly apologized to Frank Olson's family, who received $750,000 by a special act of Congress.

Though no evidence exists that the CIA succeeded in its quest to find mind-control techniques, some conspiracy theories claim that the MKULTRA project was linked to the assassination of Robert F. Kennedy. Some have argued that Kennedy's assassin, Sirhan B. Sirhan, had been subjected to mind control. Sirhan claims that he has no recollection of shooting Kennedy, despite attempts by both government prosecutors and his defense lawyers to use hypnosis to recover his memories.

# PEARL HARBOR ADVANCE KNOWLEDGE THEORY

Plenty of myths have come out of World War II, but few are as unfounded as the claim that President Franklin Delano Roosevelt allowed the Japanese to attack Pearl Harbor so the United States could enter the conflict.

Unfortunately, this rumor has followed FDR's legacy almost from the moment the attack occurred, and many people continue to believe it today. But countless investigations and studies have failed to uncover a "smoking gun" that proves the president could have engineered such a monumental act of treason.

## CODED KNOWLEDGE

Conspiracy theorists frequently note that the U.S. military had successfully broken Japanese codes and thus knew in advance of the attack. This is partially true—Japanese codes had been broken, but they were diplomatic codes, not military ones. The military *had* received notice from other sources, including the British, that an attack was pending. What wasn't known was where the attack would take place. Almost everyone assumed it would be against the Philippines or some other Pacific territory, and no one had reason to believe that the target would be the military base at Pearl Harbor.

Another common assumption is that Roosevelt had the Pacific Fleet moved from San Diego to Pearl Harbor to lure the Japanese into attacking. However, it wasn't Roosevelt who made that decision. Rather, it was the State Department, which hoped to deter Japanese aggression with a show of naval force.

## SHIPS AT SEA

Many conspiracy theorists also like to claim that the American aircraft carriers based at Pearl Harbor had been sent on maneuvers prior to the attack as a precaution, so the attack wouldn't be as damaging as it could have been. In fact, the Japanese devastated the Pacific Fleet, sinking four U.S. battleships and severely damaging four others. In addition, three light cruisers, three destroyers, and four smaller vessels were demolished or heavily damaged, and 75 percent of the island's military air fleet was annihilated before the planes could take to the sky. The value of the aircraft carriers that survived because they were on maneuvers wouldn't be realized until months later, at the Battle of Midway.

## AN EXCUSE TO FIGHT

Perhaps most important is that Roosevelt didn't need a Japanese attack to bring the United States into the war. Though officially neutral at the time, the country was actively engaged in fighting the Axis by providing war materials to Great Britain and other Allied nations via the Lend-Lease Act. Furthermore, antiwar sentiment was waning dramatically as Americans grew increasingly angered by Japanese and German aggression. It was just a matter of time before the United States took off the gloves and waded into the war that was engulfing the world.

# AREA 51

Area 51 is infamous for being the mystery spot to end all mystery spots. Speculation about its purpose runs the gamut from a top-secret test range to an alien research center. Located near the southern shore of the dry lakebed known as Groom Lake is a large military airfield—one of the most secretive places in the country. It is fairly isolated from the outside world, and little official information has ever been published on it. The area is not included on any maps, yet nearby Nevada state route 375 is listed as "The Extraterrestrial Highway." Although referred to by a variety of names, including Dreamland, Paradise Ranch, Watertown Strip, and Homey Airport, this tract of mysterious land in southern Nevada is most commonly known as "Area 51."

## AN IMPENETRABLE FORTRESS

Getting a clear idea of the size of Area 51, or even a glimpse of the place, is next to impossible. Years ago, curiosity seekers could get a good view of the facility by hiking to the top of two nearby mountain peaks known as White Sides and Freedom Ridge. But government officials soon grew weary of people climbing up there and snapping pictures, so in 1995, they seized control of both. Currently, the only way to legally catch a glimpse of the base is to scale 7,913-foot-tall Tikaboo Peak. Even if you make it that far, you're still not guaranteed to see anything because the facility is more than 25 miles away and is only visible on clear days with no haze.

The main entrance to Area 51 is along Groom Lake Road. Those brave (or foolhardy) souls who have ventured down the road to investigate quickly realize they are being watched. Video cameras and motion sensors are hidden along the road, and signs alert the curious that if they continue any further, they will be entering a military installation, which is illegal "without the written permission of the installation commander." If that's not enough to get unwanted guests to turn around, one sign clearly states: "Use of deadly force authorized." Simply put, take one step over that imaginary line in the dirt, and they will get you.

## CAMO DUDES

And just exactly who are "they"? They are the "Camo Dudes," mysterious figures watching trespassers from nearby hillsides and jeeps. If they spot something suspicious, they might call for backup—Blackhawk helicopters that will come in for a closer look. All things considered, it would probably be best to just turn around and go back home. And lest you think about hiring someone to fly you over Area 51, the entire area is considered restricted air space, meaning that unauthorized aircraft are not permitted to fly over, or even near, the facility.

## WHO WORKS THERE?

Most employees are general contractors who work for companies in the area. But rather than allow these workers to commute individually, the facility has them ushered in secretly and en masse in one of two ways. The first is a mysterious white bus with tinted windows that picks up employees at several unmarked stops before whisking them through the front gates of the facility. Every evening, the bus leaves the facility and drops the employees off.

The second mode of commuter transport, an even more secretive way, is JANET, the code name given to the secret planes that carry workers back and forth from Area 51 and Las Vegas McCarran Airport. JANET has its own terminal, which is located at the far end of the airport behind fences with special security gates. It even has its own private parking lot. Several times a day, planes from the JANET fleet take off and land at the airport.

## BOB LAZAR

The most famous Area 51 employee is someone who may or may not have actually worked there. In the late 1980s, Bob Lazar claimed that he'd worked at the secret facility he referred to as S-4. In addition, Lazar said that he was assigned the task of reverse engineering a recovered spaceship in order to determine how it worked. Lazar had only been at the facility for a short time, but he and his team had progressed to the point where they were test flying the alien spaceship. That's when Lazar made a big mistake. He decided to bring some friends out to Groom Lake Road when he knew the alien craft was being flown. He was caught and subsequently fired.

During his initial interviews with a local TV station, Lazar seemed credible and quite knowledgeable as to the inner workings of Area 51. But when people started trying to verify the information Lazar was giving, not only was it next to impossible to confirm most of his story, his education and employment history could not be verified either. Skeptics immediately proclaimed that Lazar was a fraud. To this day, Lazar contends that everything he said was factual and that the government deleted all his records in order to set him up and make him look like a fake. Whether or not he's telling the truth, Lazar will be remembered as the man who first brought up the idea that alien spaceships were being experimented on at Area 51.

## WHAT'S REALLY GOING ON?

So what really goes on inside Area 51? One thing we do know is that they work on and test aircraft. Whether they are alien spacecraft or not is still open to debate. Some of the planes worked on and tested at Area 51 include the SR-71 Blackbird and the F-117 Nighthawk stealth fighter. Currently, there are rumors that a craft known only by the code name Aurora is being worked on at the facility.

If you want to try and catch a glimpse of some of these strange craft being tested, you'll need to hang out at the "Black Mailbox" along Highway 375, also known as the Extraterrestrial Highway. It's really nothing more than a mailbox along the side of the road. But as with most things associated with Area 51, nothing is as it sounds, so it should come as no surprise that the "Black Mailbox" is actually white. It belongs to a rancher who owns the property nearby. Still, this is the spot where people have been known to camp out all night just for a chance to see something strange floating in the night sky.

## THE LAWSUIT

In 1994, a landmark lawsuit was filed against the U.S. Air Force by five unnamed contractors and the widows of two others. The suit claimed that the contractors had been present at Area 51 when large quantities of "unknown chemicals" were burned in trenches and pits. As a result of coming into contact with the fumes of the chemicals, the suit alleged that two of the contractors died, and the five survivors suffered respiratory problems and skin sores. Reporters worldwide jumped on the story, not only because it proved that Area 51 existed but also because the suit was asking for many classified documents to be entered as evidence. Would some of those documents refer to alien beings or spacecraft? The world would never know because in September 1995, while petitions for the case were still going on, President Bill Clinton signed Presidential Determination No. 95–45, which basically stated that Area 51 was exempt from federal, state, local, and interstate hazardous and solid waste laws. Shortly thereafter, the lawsuit was dismissed due to a lack of evidence, and all attempts at appeals were rejected. In 2002, President George W. Bush renewed Area 51's exemptions, ensuring once and for all that what goes on inside Area 51 stays inside Area 51.

So at the end of the day, we're still left scratching our heads about Area 51. We know it exists and we have some idea of what goes on there, but there is still so much more we don't know. More than likely, we never will know everything, but then again, what fun is a mystery if you know all the answers?

# BERMUDA TRIANGLE

Few geographical locations on Earth have been discussed and debated more than the three-sided chunk of ocean between the Atlantic coast of Florida and the regions of San Juan, Puerto Rico, and Bermuda known as the Bermuda Triangle.

Over the centuries, hundreds of ships and dozens of airplanes have mysteriously disappeared while floating in or flying through the region commonly called the Bermuda Triangle. Myth mongers propose that alien forces are responsible for these dissipations. Because little or no wreckage from the vanished vessels has ever been recovered, paranormal pirating has also been cited as the culprit. Other theorists suggest that leftover technology from the lost continent of Atlantis—mainly an underwater rock formation known as the Bimini Road (situated just off the island of Bimini in the Bahamas)—exerts a supernatural power that grabs unsuspecting intruders and drags them to the depths.

## A DEADLY ADJECTIVE

Although the theory of the Triangle had been mentioned in publications as early as 1950, it wasn't until the '60s that the region was anointed with its three-sided appellation. Columnist Vincent Gaddis wrote an article in the February 1964 edition of *Argosy* magazine that discussed the various mysterious disappearances that had occurred over the years and designated the area where myth and mystery mixed as the "Deadly Bermuda Triangle." The use of the adjective *deadly* perpetrated the possibility that UFOs, alien anarchists, supernatural beings, and metaphysical monsters reigned over the region. The mystery of Flight 19, which involved the disappearance of five planes in 1945, was first noted in newspaper articles that appeared in 1950, but its fame was secured when the flight and its fate were fictitiously featured in Steven Spielberg's 1977 alien opus, *Close Encounters of the Third Kind*. In Hollywood's view, the pilots and their planes were plucked from the sky by friendly aliens and later returned safely to terra firma by their abductors.

In 1975, historian, pilot, and researcher Lawrence David Kusche published one of the first definitive studies that dismissed many of the Triangle theories. In his book *The Bermuda Triangle Mystery—Solved*, he concluded that the Triangle was a "manufactured mystery," the result of bad research and reporting and, occasionally, deliberately falsified facts. Before weighing anchor on Kusche's conclusions, however, consider that one of his next major publications was a tome about exotic popcorn recipes.

## EXPLAINING ODD OCCURRENCES

Other pragmatists have insisted that a combination of natural forces—a double whammy of waves and rain that create the perfect storm—is most likely the cause for these maritime misfortunes. Other possible "answers" to the mysteries include rogue waves (such as the one that capsized the *Ocean Ranger* oil rig off the coast of Newfoundland in 1982), hurricanes, underwater earthquakes, and human error. The coast guard receives almost 20 distress calls every day from amateur sailors attempting to navigate the slippery sides of the Triangle. Modern-day piracy—usually among those involved in drug smuggling—has been mentioned as a probable cause for odd occurrences, as have unusual magnetic anomalies that screw up compass readings. Other possible explanations include the Gulf Stream's uncertain current, the high volume of sea and air traffic in the region, and even methane hydrates (gas bubbles) that produce "mud volcanoes" capable of sucking a ship into the depths.

# THE MYSTERY OF MONTAUK

Montauk, a beach community at the eastern tip of Long Island in New York State, has been deigned the Miami Beach of the mid-Atlantic. Conspiracy theorists, however, tell another tale. Has the U.S. government been hiding a secret at the former Camp Hero military base there?

In the late 1950s, Montauk was not the paradise-style

resort it is today. It was an isolated seaside community boasting a lighthouse commissioned by George Washington in 1792, an abandoned military base called Camp Hero, and a huge radar tower. This tower, still standing, is the last semiautomatic ground environment radar tower still in existence and features an antenna called AN/FPS-35. During its time of Air Force use, the AN/FPS-35 was capable of detecting airborne objects at a distance of more than 200 miles. One of its uses was detecting potential Soviet long-distance bombers, as the Cold War was in full swing. According to conspiracy theorists, however, the antenna and Camp Hero itself had a few other tricks lurking around the premises, namely human mind control and electromagnetic field manipulation.

## VANISHING ACT

On October 24, 1943, the USS *Eldridge* was allegedly made invisible to human sight for a brief moment as it sat in a naval shipyard in Philadelphia. The event, which has never been factually substantiated but has been sworn as true by eyewitnesses and other believers for decades, is said to have been part of a U.S. military endeavor called the Philadelphia Experiment, or Project Rainbow. Studies in electromagnetic radiation had evidenced that manipulating energy fields and bending light around objects in certain ways could render them invisible. Since the benefits to the armed forces would be incredible, the navy supposedly forged ahead with the first experiment.

There are many offshoots to the conspiracy theory surrounding the alleged event. The crew onboard the USS *Eldridge* at the time in question are said to have suffered various mental illnesses, physical ailments, and, most notably, schizophrenia, which has been medically linked to exposure to electromagnetic radiation. Some of them supposedly disappeared along with the ship and relocated through teleportation to the naval base in Norfolk, Virginia, for a moment. Despite severely conflicting eyewitness reports and the navy's assertion that the *Eldridge* wasn't even in Philadelphia that day, many Web sites, books, a video game, and a 1984 science fiction film detail the event.

But what does this have to do with Montauk right now?

## WHAT'S IN THE BASEMENT?

Camp Hero was closed as an official U.S. Army base in November 1957, although the Air Force continued to use the radar facilities. After the Air Force left in 1980, the surrounding grounds were ultimately turned into a state park, which opened to the public in September 2002. Yet the camp's vast underground facility remains under tight government jurisdiction, and the AN/FPS-35 radar tower still stands. Many say there is a government lab on-site that continues the alleged teleportation, magnetic field manipulation, and mind-control experiments that originated with Project Rainbow. One reason for this belief is that two of the sailors onboard the *Eldridge* on October 24, 1943—Al Bielek and Duncan Cameron—claimed to have jumped from the ship while it was in "hyperspace" between Philadelphia and Norfolk, and landed at Camp Hero, severely disoriented.

Though Project Rainbow was branded a hoax, an urban legend continues to surround its "legacy," which is commonly known as the Montauk Project. Theorists cite experiments in electromagnetic radiation designed to produce mass schizophrenia over time and reduce a populace's resistance to governmental control, which, they believe, would explain the continual presence of the antenna. According to these suspicions, a large number of orphans, loners, and homeless people are subjected to testing in Camp Hero's basement; most supposedly die as a result. Interestingly, some conspiracy theorists believe that one outcropping of the experiments is the emergence and popularity of the cell phone, which uses and produces electromagnetic and radio waves. Who knew that easier communication was really an evil government plot to turn people into mindless robots?

# TOP-SECRET LOCATIONS YOU CAN VISIT

There are plenty of stories of secret government facilities hidden in plain sight. Places where all sorts of strange tests take place, far away from the general public. Many of the North American top-secret government places have been (at least partially) declassified, allowing average Joes to visit. Listed here are some locations where you can play Men in Black.

## TITAN MISSILE SILO

Just a little south of Tucson, Arizona, lies the Sonoran Desert, a barren, desolate area where nothing seems to be happening. That's exactly why, during the Cold War, the U.S. government hid an underground Titan Missile silo there.

Inside the missile silo, one of dozens that once littered the area, a Titan 2 Missile could be armed and launched in just under 90 seconds. Until it was finally abandoned in the 1990s, the government manned the silo 24 hours a day, with every member being trained to "turn the key" and launch the missile at a moment's notice. Today, the silo is open to the public as the Titan Missile Museum. Visitors can take a look at one of the few remaining Titan 2 missiles in existence, still sitting on the launch pad (relax, it's been disarmed). Folks with extra dough can also spend the night inside the silo and play the role of one of the crew members assigned to prepare to launch the missile at a moment's notice.

## PEANUT ISLAND

You wouldn't think a sunny place called Peanut Island, located near Palm Beach, Florida, could hold many secrets. Yet in December 1961, the U.S. Navy came to the island on a secret mission to create a fallout shelter for then-President John F. Kennedy and his family. The shelter was completed, but it was never used and was all but forgotten when the Cold War ended. Today, the shelter is maintained by the Palm Beach Maritime Museum, which conducts weekend tours of the space.

## LOS ALAMOS NATIONAL LABORATORY

Until recently, the U.S. government refused to acknowledge the Los Alamos National Laboratory's existence. But in the early 1940s, the lab was created near Los Alamos, New Mexico, to develop the first nuclear weapons in what would become known as the Manhattan Project. Back then, the facility was so top secret it didn't even have a name. It was simply referred to as Site Y. No matter what it was called, the lab produced two nuclear bombs, nicknamed Little Boy and Fat Man—bombs that would be dropped on Hiroshima and Nagasaki, Japan, effectively ending World War II. Today, tours of portions of the facility can be arranged through the Lab's Public Affairs Department.

## FORT KNOX

It is the stuff that legends are made of: A mythical building filled with over 4,700 tons of gold, stacked up and piled high to the ceiling. But this is no fairytale—the gold really does exist, and it resides inside Fort Knox.

Since 1937, the U.S. Department of the Treasury's Bullion Depository has been storing the gold inside Fort Knox on a massive military campus that stretches across three counties in north-central Kentucky. Parts of the campus are open for tours, including the General George Patton Museum. But don't think you're going to catch a glimpse of that shiny stuff—visitors are not permitted to go through the gate or enter the building.

# HANGAR 18

Even those who aren't UFO buffs have probably heard about the infamous Roswell Incident, where an alien spaceship supposedly crash-landed in the New Mexico desert, and the U.S. government covered the whole thing up. But what most people don't know is that according to legend, the mysterious aircraft was recovered (along with some alien bodies), secreted out of Roswell, and came to rest just outside of Dayton, Ohio.

## SOMETHING CRASHED IN THE DESERT

While the exact date is unclear, sometime during the first week of July 1947, a local Roswell rancher by the name of Mac Brazel decided to go out and check his property for fallen trees and other damage after a night of heavy storms and lightning. Brazel allegedly came across an area of his property littered with strange debris unlike anything he had ever seen before. Some of the debris even had strange writing on it.

Brazel showed some of the debris to a few neighbors and then took it to the office of Roswell Sheriff George Wilcox, who called authorities at Roswell Army Air Field. After speaking with Wilcox, intelligence officer Major Jesse Marcel drove out to the Brazel ranch and collected as much debris as he could. He then returned to the airfield and showed the debris to his commanding officer, Colonel William Blanchard, commander of the 509th Bomb Group that was stationed at the Roswell Air Field. Upon seeing the debris, Blanchard dispatched military vehicles and personnel back out to the Brazel ranch to see if they could recover anything else.

## "FLYING SAUCER CAPTURED!"

On July 8, 1947, Colonel Blanchard issued a press release stating that the wreckage of a "crashed disk" had been recovered. The bold headline of the July 8 edition of the *Roswell Daily Record* read: "RAAF Captures Flying Saucer on Ranch in Roswell Region." Newspapers around the world ran similar headlines. But then, within hours of the Blanchard release, General Roger M. Ramey, commander of the Eighth Air Force in Fort Worth, Texas, retracted Blanchard's release for him and issued another statement saying there was no UFO. Blanchard's men had simply recovered a fallen weather balloon.

Before long, the headlines that had earlier touted the capture of a UFO read: "It's a Weather Balloon" and "'Flying Disc' Turns Up as Just Hot Air." Later editions even ran a staged photograph of Major Jesse Marcel, who was first sent to investigate the incident, kneeling in front of weather balloon debris. Most of the general public seemed content with the explanation, but there were skeptics.

## WHISKED AWAY TO HANGAR 18?

Those who believe that aliens crash-landed near Roswell claim that, under cover of darkness, large portions of the alien spacecraft were brought out to the Roswell Air Field and loaded onto B-29 and C-54 aircrafts. Those planes were then supposedly flown to Wright-Patterson Air Force Base, just outside of Dayton, Ohio. Once the planes landed, they were taxied over to Hangar 18 and unloaded. And according to legend, it's all still there.

There are some problems with the story, though. For one, none of the hangars on Wright-Patterson Air Force Base are officially known as "Hangar 18," and there are no buildings designated with the number 18. Rather, the hangars are labeled 1A, 1B, 1C, and so on.

There's also the fact that none of the hangars seem large enough to house and conceal an alien spacecraft. But just because there's nothing listed as Hangar 18 on a Wright-Patterson map doesn't mean it's not there. Conspiracy theorists believe that hangars 4A, 4B, and 4C might be the infamous Hangar 18. As for the overall size of the hangars, it's believed that most of the wreckage has been stored in giant underground tunnels and chambers deep under the hangar, both to protect the debris and to keep it safe from prying eyes. It is said that Wright-Patterson is currently conducting experiments on the wreckage to see if scientists can reverse-engineer the technology.

## SO WHAT'S THE DEAL?

The story of Hangar 18 only got stranger as the years went on, starting with the government's Project Blue Book, a program designed to investigate reported UFO sightings across the United States. Between 1947 and 1969, Project

Blue Book investigated more than 12,000 UFO sightings before being disbanded. And where was Project Blue Book headquartered? Wright-Patterson Air Force Base.

Then in the early 1960s, Arizona Senator Barry Goldwater, himself a retired major general in the U.S. Army Air Corps (and a friend of Colonel Blanchard), became interested in what, if anything, had crashed in Roswell. When Goldwater discovered Hangar 18, he first wrote directly to Wright-Patterson and asked for permission to tour the facility but was quickly denied. He then approached another friend, General Curtis LeMay, and asked if he could see the "Green Room" where the UFO secret was being held. Goldwater claimed that LeMay gave him "holy hell" and screamed at Goldwater, "Not only can't you get into it, but don't you ever mention it to me again."

In 1982, retired pilot Oliver "Pappy" Henderson attended a reunion and announced that he was one of the men who had flown alien bodies out of Roswell in a C-54 cargo plane. His destination? Hangar 18 at Wright-Patterson. Although no one is closer to a definitive answer, it seems that the legend of Hangar 18 will never die.

# VANISHED: THE LOST COLONY OF ROANOKE ISLAND

Twenty years before England established its first successful colony in the New World, an entire village of English colonists disappeared in what would later be known as North Carolina. Did these pioneers all perish? Did Native Americans capture them? Did they join a friendly tribe? Could they have left descendants who live among us today?

## TIMING IS EVERYTHING

Talk about bad timing. As far as John White was concerned, England couldn't have picked a worse time to go to war. It was November 1587, and White had just arrived in England from the New World. He intended to gather relief supplies and immediately sail back to Roanoke Island, where he had left more than 100 colonists who were running short of food. Unfortunately, the English were gearing up to fight Spain. Every seaworthy ship, including White's, was pressed into naval service. Not a one could be spared for his return voyage to America.

## NOBODY HOME

When John White finally returned to North America three years later, he was dismayed to discover that the colonists he had left behind were nowhere to be found. Instead, he stumbled upon a mystery—one that has never been solved.

The village that White and company had founded in 1587 on Roanoke Island lay completely deserted. Houses had been dismantled (as if someone planned to move them), but the pieces lay in the long grass along with iron tools and farming equipment. A stout stockade made of logs stood empty.

White found no sign of his daughter Eleanor, her husband Ananias, or their daughter Virginia Dare—the first English child born in America. None of the 87 men, 17 women, and 11 children remained. No bodies or obvious gravesites offered clues to their fate. The only clues—if they were clues—that White could find were the letters CRO carved into a tree trunk and the word CROATOAN carved into a log of the abandoned fort.

## NO FORWARDING ADDRESS

All White could do was hope that the colonists had been taken in by friendly natives.

Croatoan—also spelled "Croatan"—was the name of a barrier island to the south and also the name of a tribe of Native Americans that lived on that island. Unlike other area tribes, the Croatoans had been friendly to English newcomers, and one of them, Manteo, had traveled to England with earlier explorers and returned to act as interpreter for the Roanoke colony. Had the colonists, with Manteo's help, moved to Croatoan? Were they safe among friends?

White tried to find out, but his timing was rotten once again. He had arrived on the Carolina coast as a hurricane bore down on the region. The storm hit before he could mount a search. His ship was blown past Croatoan Island and out to sea. Although the ship and crew survived the storm and made it back to England, White was stuck again. He tried repeatedly but failed to raise money for another search party.

No one has ever learned the fate of the Roanoke Island colonists, but there is no shortage of theories as to what happened to them. A small sailing vessel and other boats that White had left with them were gone when he returned. It's possible that the colonists used the vessels to travel to another island or to the mainland. White had talked with others before he left about possibly moving the settlement to a more secure location inland. It's even possible that the colonists tired of waiting for White's return and tried to sail back to England. If so, they would have perished at sea. Yet there are at least a few shreds of hearsay evidence that the colonists survived in America.

## RUMORS OF SURVIVORS

In 1607, Captain John Smith and company established the first successful English settlement in North America at Jamestown, Virginia. The colony's secretary, William Strachey, wrote four years later about hearing a report of four English men, two boys, and one young woman who had been sighted south of Jamestown at a settlement of the Eno tribe, where they were being used as slaves. If the report was true, who else could these English have been but Roanoke survivors?

For more than a century after the colonists' disappearance, stories emerged of gray-eyed Native Americans and English-speaking villages in North Carolina and Virginia. In 1709, an English surveyor said members of the Hatteras tribe living on North Carolina's Outer Banks—some of them with light-colored eyes—claimed to be descendants of white people. It's possible that the Hatteras were the same people that the 1587 colonists called Croatoan.

In the intervening centuries, many of the individual tribes of the region have disappeared. Some died out. Others were absorbed into larger groups such as the Tuscarora. One surviving group, the Lumbee, has also been called Croatoan. The Lumbee, who still live in North Carolina, often have Caucasian features. Could they be descendants of Roanoke colonists? Many among the Lumbee dismiss the notion as fanciful, but the tribe has long been thought to be of mixed heritage and has been speaking English so long that none among them know what language preceded it.

# CRYBABY BRIDGES ACROSS AMERICA

Located throughout the United States, crybaby bridges are

said to mark locations where a baby died. And, according to legend, if you're brave enough to wait patiently on the bridge, you'll actually hear the baby cry. Here are some of the most popular crybaby bridges across the United States.

## MIDDLETOWN, NEW JERSEY

Cooper Road is a lonely stretch of road that wanders through the backwoods of Middletown. Stay on this road long enough and you will eventually come to the crybaby bridge under which a baby is said to have drowned. If you want to hear the baby cry, just position your vehicle in the middle of the bridge and wait. But make sure you don't turn your car off or you won't be able to start it again.

## MONMOUTH, ILLINOIS

It's a case of "the more the scarier" for this crybaby bridge in western Illinois. According to legend, an entire busload of small children drove off the bridge when the driver lost control. It is said that if you go to the bridge at night, turn off your car's engine, and put your vehicle in neutral, you'll hear cries from the dead children. Shortly thereafter, ghostly hands will push your car across the bridge and back onto the road, leaving tiny handprints on the back of your car.

## CONCORD, NORTH CAROLINA

Just outside of Concord is a bridge on Poplar Tent Road that locals refer to as Sally's Bridge. According to local lore, a young woman named Sally was driving home with her baby when she lost control of her car, skidded across the bridge, and crashed. The baby was ejected from the vehicle and fell into the water. Panic-stricken, Sally dove into the water to try to save her child, but sadly both mother and child drowned.

Today, legend has it that Sally's ghost will bang on your car, desperately trying to find someone to help save her dying child.

## UPPER MARLBORO, MARYLAND

The story associated with this crybaby bridge says that a young, single woman became pregnant. Embarrassed and afraid of being disowned, she somehow managed to conceal her pregnancy from her family and friends. When the baby was born, the woman waited until nightfall, walked out to the bridge, then threw the baby from the bridge into the water below. Legend has it that if you go out to the bridge at night, you'll hear the baby crying.

## CABLE, OHIO

Far and away, Ohio harbors the most crybaby bridges, each with its own unique spin on the classic crybaby bridge story. For example, legend has it that on a cold November night in the tiny town of Cable, a deeply depressed woman bundled up her newborn baby and walked onto a bridge that crossed over some railroad tracks. She waited patiently until she heard the sound of a distant train whistle. With the baby still in her arms, the woman jumped in front of the oncoming train just as it reached the bridge. Both were killed instantly.

If you visit this bridge, be forewarned—especially when it's close to midnight. Unlucky travelers crossing the bridge at that time have reported that their cars suddenly stalled. When they tried to restart the engines, they heard the sound of a distant train whistle, which seemed to signal the start of a bizarre and ghostly flashback. As the whistle got closer, motorists reported hearing a baby crying. Then, just when it sounded as though the train was right next to the bridge, they heard a woman scream…and then everything went silent. Only then were they able to start their cars again.

# BIGFOOT: THE KING OF ALL MONSTERS

Let's face it—if you had to pick one monster that stands head (and feet) above all others, it would be Bigfoot. Not only is it the stuff of legends, but its likeness has also been used to promote everything from pizza to beef jerky. Bigfoot has had amusement park rides and monster trucks named after it and was even slated to be one of the mascots for the 2010 Winter Olympics in Vancouver, British Columbia.

## EARLY SIGHTINGS

Folktales from Native American tribes throughout the Northwest, the area that Bigfoot traditionally calls home, are filled with references to giant, apelike creatures roaming the woods. They described the beast as between seven and ten feet tall and covered in brown or dark hair. (*Sasquatch*, a common term used for the big-footed beast, is actually an anglicization of a Native American term for a giant supernatural creature.)

Walking on two legs, there was something humanlike about Sasquatch's appearance, although its facial features more closely resembled that of an ape, and it had almost no neck. With looks like that, it's not surprising that Native American folklore often described the creature as cannibalistic, supernatural, and dangerous. Other tales, however, said Sasquatch appeared to be frightened of humans and mostly kept to itself.

It wasn't until the 1900s, when more and more woodlands were being devoured in the name of progress, that Sasquatch sightings started to increase. It was believed that, though generally docile, the beast did have a mean streak when feeling threatened. In July 1924, Fred Beck and several others were mining in a mountainous area of Washington State. One evening, the group spotted and shot at what appeared to be an apelike creature. After fleeing to their cabin, the group was startled when several more hairy giants began banging on the walls, windows, and doors. For several hours, the creatures pummeled the cabin and threw large rocks at it before disappearing shortly before dawn. After several such encounters in the same general vicinity, the area was renamed Ape Canyon.

## MY, WHAT BIG FEET YOU HAVE!

In August 1958, Jerry Crew, a bulldozer operator, showed up for work at a wooded site in Bluff Creek, California. Walking up to his bulldozer, which had been left there overnight, Crew found giant footprints in the dirt. At first, they appeared to be the naked footprints of a man, but with one major difference—these feet were huge! After the tracks appeared on several occasions, Crew took a cast of one of them and brought it to *The Humboldt Times* in Eureka, California. The following day, the newspaper ran a front-page story, complete with photos of the footprint and a name for the creature: Bigfoot. The story and photographs hit the Associated Press, and the name stuck.

Even so, the event is still rife with controversy. Skeptics claim that it was Ray Wallace, not Bigfoot, who made the tracks as a practical joke on his brother Wilbur, who was Crew's supervisor. Apparently the joke backfired when Crew arrived at the site first and saw the prints before Wilbur. However, Ray Wallace never admitted to faking the tracks or having anything to do with perpetrating a hoax.

## VIDEO EVIDENCE?

In 1967, in response to numerous Bigfoot sightings in

northern California, Roger Patterson rented a 16mm video camera in hopes of filming the elusive creature. Patterson and his friend Robert Gimlin spent several days on horseback traveling though the Six Rivers National Forest without coming across as much a footprint.

Then, on October 20, the pair rounded a bend and noticed something dark and hairy crouched near the water. When the creature stood up on two legs and presented itself in all its hairy, seven-foot glory, that's when Patterson said he knew for sure he was looking at Bigfoot. Unfortunately, Patterson's horse saw the creature, too, and suddenly reared up. Because of this, it took Patterson several precious seconds to get off the horse and remove the video camera from his saddlebag. Once he did that, he ran toward the creature, filming as he went.

As the creature walked away, Patterson continued filming until his tape ran out. He quickly changed his film, and then both men retrieved their frightened horses and attempted to follow Bigfoot further before eventually losing sight of it.

When they arrived back in town, Patterson reviewed the film. Even though it was less than a minute long and extremely shaky in spots, the film appeared to show Bigfoot running away while occasionally looking toward the camera. For most Bigfoot enthusiasts, the Patterson-Gimlin film stands as the Holy Grail of Bigfoot sightings—physical proof captured on video. Skeptics, however, alleged that Patterson and Gimlin faked the entire incident and filmed a man in an expensive monkey suit. Nevertheless, more than 40 years after the event occurred, the Patterson-Gimlin film is still one of the most talked about pieces of Bigfoot evidence, mainly because neither man ever admitted to a hoax and the fact that no one has been able to figure out how they faked it.

### GONE SASQUATCHING

The fact that some people doubt the existence of Bigfoot hasn't stopped thousands of people from heading into the woods to try to find one. Even today, the hairy creature makes brief appearances here and there. Of course, sites like YouTube have given rise to dozens of "authentic" videos of Bigfoot, some of which are quite comical.

Still, every once in a while, a video that deserves a second look pops up. For example, in 2005, ferry operator Bobby Clarke filmed almost three minutes of video of a Bigfoot-like creature on the banks of the Nelson River in Manitoba. And in late 2007, photos taken by a hunter in Pennsylvania's Allegheny National Forest were being analyzed.

# SPOTTING SASQUATCH

Throughout the world, it's called Alma, Yeti, Sasquatch, the Abominable Snowman, Wildman, and Bigfoot. Whatever the name, people agree that it's tall, hairy, doesn't smell good, and has a habit of showing up in locations around the globe—especially in North America.

### WANOGA BUTTE, OREGON (1957)

After a long, uneventful morning hunting, Gary Joanis and Jim Newall were ecstatic when Joanis felled a deer with a single shot. But when a hairy creature "not less than nine feet tall" emerged from the woods, threw the deer over its shoulder, and lumbered off, the two men were left speechless.

# MONROE, MICHIGAN (1965)

On August 13, Christine Van Acker and her mother were driving when a large, hairy creature came out of the nearby woods. Frightened by the creature, the mother lost control of the car and grazed the beast. The car stalled and while the mother struggled to start it, the creature put its arm through the window, struck Christine in the face and slammed her mother's head against the car door, leaving both women with black eyes, photos of which were widely circulated in the press.

# SPEARFISH, SOUTH DAKOTA (1977)

Betty Johnson and her three daughters saw two Bigfoot in a cornfield. The larger of the two was eight-feet tall; the other, slightly smaller. They both appeared to be eating corn and making a whistling sound.

# PARIS TOWNSHIP, OHIO (1978)

Herbert and Evelyn Cayton reported that a seven-foot-tall, 300-pound, fur-covered creature appeared at their house so frequently that their daughter thought it was a pet.

# JACKSON, WYOMING (1980)

On June 17, Glenn Towner and Robert Goodrich went into the woods on Snow King Mountain to check out a lean-to built by a friend of theirs. After hearing moaning and growling, the pair was chased out of the woods by a 12-foot-tall creature covered in hair. The creature followed them back to civilization, where it was last spotted standing briefly beneath a streetlight before vanishing back into the woods.

## CRESCENT CITY, CALIFORNIA (1995)

A TV crew was driving in their RV, filming the scenery in Jedediah Smith Redwoods State Park, when an eight-foot-tall hairy giant crossed their path and was caught on tape.

## COTTON ISLAND, LOUISIANA (2000)

Bigfoot surprised lumberjacks Earl Whitstine and Carl Dubois while they were clearing timber. The hairy figure returned a few days later, leaving behind footprints and hair samples.

## SELMA, OREGON (2000)

While hiking with his family near the Oregon Caves National Monument on July 1, psychologist Matthew Johnson smelled a strange musky odor. Hearing odd grunting noises coming from behind some trees, Johnson went to investigate and saw something very tall and hairy walking away. When asked to describe it, Johnson said that it could be "nothing else but a Sasquatch."

## GRANTON, WISCONSIN (2000)

As James Hughes was delivering newspapers early one morning, he saw a shaggy figure, about eight feet tall, carrying a goat. However, sheriffs called to the scene couldn't find any footprints or missing goats.

## MT. ST. HELENS, WASHINGTON (2002)

Jerry Kelso made his wife and two-year-old child wait in the car while he chased what he thought was a man in a gorilla suit. When he was about 100 feet away, he realized that it wasn't a gorilla suit and that the seven-foot-tall creature was carrying a club.

# HOLLYWOOD'S URBAN LEGENDS

They say that truth is stranger than fiction. Nowhere is that more obvious than in Hollywood, where legends are born... and some really great urban legends are, too!

## HUMPHREY BOGART WAS THE GERBER BABY

Everyone knows the famous black-and-white drawing of the baby that graces Gerber baby food products. Well, there's an urban legend that the baby is none other than actor Humphrey Bogart. This legend probably took off due to the fact that Bogart's mother, Maud, was a commercial illustrator who actually did sell drawings of her son to advertising agencies. In fact, she did allow one of her drawings of Humphrey to be used in a baby food advertisement— for Mellin's Baby Food. However, Gerber did not start producing baby food until 1928, and by that time, Bogart was 29 years old, making it unlikely—but not impossible— that Bogart could be the Gerber baby. We now know that Ann Turner Cook was the lucky model in 1928. Artist Dorothy Hope Smith, who submitted the drawing to Gerber, drew her.

## WALT DISNEY ON ICE

In life, Walt Disney warmed the hearts of millions. In death, Disney is rumored to have had himself frozen until such a time that scientists could warm him up and bring him back to life. What sounds like something out of a sci-fi movie may have been rooted in the fact that Walt Disney liked to keep his personal life private, so when he died, specifics about his burial were kept under wraps, leading to all sorts of speculation. Rumors were further fueled when Disney was buried in Forest Lawn Cemetery in Glendale, California, which does not publicly list who is interred there. But Walt Disney's unfrozen remains are indeed there, in the Freedom Mausoleum, along with those of several family members.

## THREE MEN AND A BABY...AND A GHOST!

There's a scene in the movie *Three Men and a Baby* (1987) in which Ted Danson's character, Jack, and his mother are walking through Jack's house while the mother is holding the baby. As they walk in front of a window, the ghostly image of a boy is seen standing in the background. When the characters walk by the window a second time, the boy has been replaced by what appears to be a shotgun. Legend has it that the ghost belongs to a boy who accidentally shot himself to death with a shotgun in the house where the movie was filmed.

Of course, the truth is a little less spooky. What many people mistake for the boy's apparition is nothing more than a cardboard cutout of Danson, which was supposed to be part of a subplot involving Jack's appearance in a dog food commercial. And those scenes weren't filmed in a house, either. They all took place on a studio set in Toronto.

## MUNCHKIN SUICIDE IN THE WIZARD OF OZ

In *The Wizard of Oz* (1939), shortly after Dorothy and the Scarecrow convince the Tin Man to join their posse, they begin singing and skipping down the Yellow Brick Road. As they round the bend in the road and dance off the screen, a strange, dark shape can be seen moving in a bizarre fashion to the left of the road. It is said that one of the Munchkins, heartbroken over a failed love affair, chose to take his own life as the cameras rolled. It makes for a creepy story, but there's no truth to it. What people are actually seeing is nothing more than an exotic bird flapping its wings. Prior to filming, the director decided that adding strange, exotic birds to the scene would add a bit more color, so he rented several such birds from the Los Angeles Zoo and allowed them to roam freely about the set.

## DISNEY'S SNUFF FILM

In the 1958 Disney documentary *White Wilderness*, dozens of lemmings are shown jumping to their deaths off a cliff into the ocean as part of a bizarre suicide ritual. There was only one glitch: Lemmings don't commit suicide en masse. When principal photographer James R. Simon arrived in Alberta, Canada, to film, he was informed of this. But rather than scrap the project, Simon had the lemmings herded up and forced off the cliff while the cameras rolled. As the creatures struggled to keep from drowning, the narrator delivered the disturbing and all-too-telling line: "It's not given to man to understand all of nature's mysteries."

Despite the film winning an Oscar for Best Documentary in 1959, once the truth about what happened on those cliffs was revealed, it quickly and quietly was locked away, becoming one of Disney's deep, dark secrets.

# MERMAIDS: REAL OR FISH-CTION?

The idea that mermaids actually exist is, well, a bit fishy. But anyone who has ever watched *The Little Mermaid* or *Splash* knows that there's a magic surrounding mermaids that is irresistible. And now a Discovery Channel documentary has stunned viewers with their suggestion that the answer is "maybe."

The earliest image of a mermaid comes from 1000 B.C. in Syria, where the goddess Atargatis tried to take on the form of a fish by diving into the sea. She was not allowed to give up her great beauty, however, and the result was half fish and half human—a goddess of the sea with a beautiful face, long flowing hair, and the sleek glimmering tale of a fish.

Homer's *The Odyssey* expanded on that idea by creating half human sea creatures called "sirens." Beautiful? Yes. But a little evil as well. These mermaids sang harmonious tunes, luring sailors to their death in the sea.

Stories of their existence have been told and retold for a couple thousand years. And artists have depicted the mythical creatures in their artwork for just as long. Almost every country and culture has tales of mermaids and many people claim to have seen one. It begs the question: before mass communication as we know it today, how did all these separate cultures come up with the same imaginary creature with so many of the same characteristics?

## COULD THEY BE REAL?

The answer is maybe. The Discovery Channel program follows the scientific investigation of two former National Oceanic Atmospheric Administration (NOAA) scientists who started out to learn more about the beaching of whales in 2007. What they discovered were some mysterious underwater sounds—like nothing they had ever heard before.

Underwater singing? There must be mermaids! Well, it wasn't quite that simple, but the team did feel that the noises merited additional investigation—especially since they were convinced that this mysterious creature was attempting to communicate with them.

When another whale beaching occurred along the coast of South Africa, the scientists traveled there and found that African scientists had recorded similar underwater communications. Further investigation revealed the remains of this sea creature in the belly of a great white shark—and it was definitely a marine animal. And a human. In short, it appeared to be a mermaid.

This creature was not a Disney princess by any means. But it did appear to possess the tail of a fish along with the clearly defined hands associated with the human body. If nothing else, this unusual creature supported an old "aquatic ape" theory about ancient mammals that lived on both land and sea. But alas, the government took possession of these remains, leaving the scientists with nothing but their recording of an unusual sea-sound.

As is often the case with government actions, their decision to confiscate the remains only convinced the scientists—and everyone hearing the story—that they were on to something. They tracked down a local teenager who claimed to have seen the body of a mermaid on the beach along with the whales. And surprise—he had taken a video with his cell phone.

Unfortunately the video wasn't clear and the government denies any discovery or cover-up of mermaids. NOAA has also issued a statement saying there's no evidence that "aquatic humanoids" have ever been found. And the Discovery Channel admits that their show was meant to entertain—while it shows how mermaids could be real, it was as much science fiction as science.

So are there mermaids? Maybe.

# DO VACCINES CAUSE AUTISM?

Do vaccines cause autism? This has become one of the most pernicious and destructive myths of modern times. Imagine the horrified faces of historical people whose children died of scarlet fever when they find out childhood diseases have reemerged, especially affecting the children whose weakened immune systems mean they can't be vaccinated at all.

## NO LINK AT ALL

Study after study has shown that there is no link *at all* between vaccines of any kind and autism. For those who rely on celebrities for their parenting advice, there are plenty of dumb unqualified actors who are paid to play pretend as a job who are on board with all kinds of conspiracy theories.

Most Americans are not very scientifically literate in the first place, but groups with higher numbers of fine-arts degrees may be even less so, and certainly aren't *more* qualified to speak to our health concerns. A registered nurse, with at least a bachelor's degree in science and healthcare and a standardized qualification, isn't allowed to prescribe medication—some Internet celebrity should not tell you that colloid silver and powdered mushrooms will prevent cancer, or that a pendant will ease your back pain.

## ROLLING THE MEDICAL CLOCK BACKWARD

The vaccine conspiracy began with a radically misguided and mistaken physician who was stripped of his license over the sheer dangerous incorrectness of his terrible work. His study was not statistically significant or rigorous, it isn't duplicable, and it has been disproven thousands of times since.

He has doubled down on his claims, and he maintains a business that seems to just be his followers giving him money directly. And he has created a confirmation-bias echo chamber where the fact that he's shunned by the medical industry means he must "really be onto something." His fearmongering has resonated with modern parents who are in the center of a terrible Venn diagram where everything they choose is judged by other parents, every media outlet harps on how allegedly dangerous chemicals are coating our entire lives, and every decision they make feels like a moment when they can permanently damage their children.

## LIMITS OF SKEPTICISM

It's completely understandable to be bewildered and feel skeptical and look for answers. The best source for those answers is the world of trained, educated, and certified medical professionals. Even a staggered immunization schedule, which many anti-vaccine activists choose as a "compromise," can leave their and other children vulnerable to diseases. As herd immunity falls in communities where anti-vaccine activists gather, immune-compromised children are the first to suffer.

# PHANTOM HITCHHIKERS

The tale of the vanishing hitchhiker is an urban legend—an account of something that usually happened to a "friend of a friend of a friend" (almost never to the person telling the story) that typically contains some kind of moral or surprise ending. According to Jan Harold Brunvand, who has written numerous books about urban legends, the story of the vanishing hitchhiker is one that has been reported in newspapers and elsewhere since at least the 1930s, and possibly earlier. Are any of these anecdotes true? That's for you to decide.

## THE HITCHHIKER'S TALE

The basic story goes like this: A motorist driving down a country road sees a young lady hitchhiking, so he stops to offer her a ride. The girl tells him that she lives in a house a few miles down the road, but she is otherwise uncommunicative, spending most of the drive staring out the window. When they arrive at the house, the driver turns to his passenger, only to find that she has disappeared. Curious, he knocks on the door of the house and tells the person who answers about his experience. The homeowner says that he or she had a daughter who fit the description of the hitchhiker, but that she disappeared (or died) several years earlier while hitchhiking on the road on which the driver found the girl. The parent tells the driver that, coincidentally, it's the daughter's birthday.

The specifics of this tale often vary. For example, sometimes a married couple picks up the ghostly hitchhiker, and sometimes the hitchhiker is a young man. However, the story's shocking ending is almost always the same.

## IN THE EARLY DAYS

The legend of Chicago's Resurrection Mary is perhaps the earliest "phantom hitchhiker" story. Another early account of a vanishing hitchhiker was first told sometime between 1935 and 1941. A traveling salesman from Spartanburg, South Carolina, stopped for a woman who was walking along the side of a road. The woman told the man that she was going to her brother's house, which was about three miles up the road. The man offered to give her a ride and encouraged her to sit next to him, but the woman would only sit in the backseat. They talked briefly, but soon the woman grew quiet. Upon arriving at the home of the woman's brother, the driver turned to the backseat, only to find it empty. The driver told the woman's brother his story, but the brother didn't seem surprised: He said that the woman was his sister and that she had died two years earlier. Several drivers had picked her up on that road, but she had yet to reach the house.

Like all good stories, the tale of the vanishing hitchhiker often acquires some unique details with each retelling. In one example collected by Brunvand, the female hitchhiker suddenly pulled the car's emergency brake at a particular intersection, preventing a deadly collision; the driver was momentarily shaken, but when he finally remembered his passenger, she was gone—though she had left a book in the backseat. (In other accounts, the object is a purse, a sweater, or a scarf.) The driver assumed that she simply got out so that she could walk the rest of the way. Regardless, he drove to the intended destination, where the homeowner told him that the girl the driver had picked up was his daughter, who had died in a car accident at the same intersection where the collision had been averted. Taking the book from the driver, the father went to his library, where he found an empty space where the book should have been.

The story of the vanishing hitchhiker may only be an urban legend—a story designed to shock the listener—but when dealing with the paranormal, who can be sure? Keep that in mind the next time you spot a young lady hitchhiking along the side of the road.

## MONSTER ON THE CHESAPEAKE

Chesapeake Bay, a 200-mile intrusion of the Atlantic Ocean into Virginia and Maryland, is 12 miles wide at its mouth, allowing plenty of room for strange saltwater creatures to slither on in. Encounters with giant, serpentine beasts up and down the Eastern seaboard were reported during the 1800s, but sightings of Chessie, a huge, snakelike creature with a football-shape head and flippers began to escalate in the 1960s. Former CIA employee Donald Kyker and some neighbors saw not one, but four unidentified water creatures swimming near shore in 1978.

Then in 1980, the creature was spotted just off Love Point, sparking a media frenzy. Two years later, Maryland resident Robert Frew was entertaining dinner guests with his wife, Karen, when the whole party noticed a giant water creature about 200 yards from shore swimming toward a group of people frolicking nearby in the surf. They watched the creature, which they estimated to be about 30 feet in length, as it dove underneath the unsuspecting humans, emerged on the other side, and swam away.

Frew recorded several minutes of the creature's antics, and the Smithsonian Museum of Natural History reviewed his film. Although they could not identify the animal, they did concede that it was "animate," or living.

## THE CHESSIE CHALLENGE

Some believe Chessie is a manatee, but they usually swim in much warmer waters and are only about ten feet long. Also, the fact that Chessie is often seen with several "humps" breaking the water behind its head leads other investigators to conclude that it could be either a giant sea snake or a large seal.

One Maryland resident has compiled a list of 78 different sightings over the years. And a tour boat operator offers sea-monster tours in hopes of repeating the events of 1980 when 25 passengers on several charter boats all spotted Chessie cavorting in the waves.

# SATANIC MARKETING

What's behind the vicious rumor that put mega-corporation Procter & Gamble on many churches' hit lists?

Procter & Gamble, one of the largest corporations in the world, manufactures a plethora of products that range from pet food to potato chips. The company takes pride in its reputation as a business that can be trusted, so it came as a huge shock when, starting in the 1960s, Christian churches and individuals around the country spread the rumor that P&G was dedicated to the service of Satan.

## THE DEVIL IS IN THE DETAILS

How the rumor got started remains a mystery. According to one of the most popular versions of the story, the president of P&G appeared on *The Phil Donahue Show* in March 1994 and announced that, because of society's new openness, he finally felt comfortable revealing that he was a member of the Church of Satan and that much of his company's profits went toward the advancement of that organization. When Donahue supposedly asked him whether such an announcement would have a negative impact on P&G, the CEO replied, "There aren't enough Christians in the United States to make a difference."

There's one problem with this story—and with the variations that place the company president on *The Sally Jessy Raphael Show*, *The Merv Griffin Show*, and *60 Minutes*: It didn't happen.

## LOSE THE LOGO

Adding fuel to the fable was the company's logo, which featured the image of a "man in the moon" and 13 stars. Many interpreted this rather innocuous design to be Satanic, and some even claimed that the curlicues in the man's beard looked like the number 666—the biblical "mark of the Beast" referred to in the Book of Revelation. By 1985, the company had become so frustrated by the allegations that it had no choice but to retire the logo, which had graced P&G products for more than 100 years.

## SPEAKING OUT

Procter & Gamble did all it could to quell the rumors, which resulted in more than 200,000 phone calls and letters from concerned consumers. Company spokespeople vehemently denied the story, explaining in a press release: "The president of P&G has never discussed Satanism on any national televised talk show, nor has any other P&G executive. The moon-and-stars trademark dates back to the mid-1800s, when the 'man in the moon' was simply a popular design. The 13 stars in the design honor the original 13 colonies."

In addition, the company turned to several prominent religious leaders, including evangelist Billy Graham, to help clear its name, and when that didn't work, it even sued a handful of clergy members who continued to spread the offending story.

Talk show host Sally Jessy Raphael also denied the allegations, noting, "The rumors going around that the president of Procter & Gamble appeared on [my] show and announced he was a member of the Church of Satan are not true. The president of Procter & Gamble has never appeared on *The Sally Jessy Raphael Show*."

## SENSELESS ALLEGATIONS

Of course, like most urban legends, this story falls apart under the slightest scrutiny. Foremost, one must ask why the CEO of an international conglomerate (especially one that must answer to stockholders) would risk decades of consumer goodwill—not to mention billions of dollars in sales—to announce to the world that his company was run by and catered to Satanists. And even if that were the case, he needn't bother announcing it, since any deals made with the devil would be a matter of public record.

In 2007, a jury awarded Procter & Gamble $19.25 million in a civil lawsuit filed against four former Amway distributors accused of spreading false rumors about the company's ties to the Church of Satan. The distributors were found guilty of using a voicemail system to inform customers that P&G's profits were used to support Satanic cults.

# TIME TRAVELERS

Hold on to your hat—you're in for a wild, mind-blowing ride back and forth through the realms of time!

In 2013, many people didn't believe President Obama when he claimed that he often fired guns on the skeet shooting range at Camp David. But others believed that Obama had actually come close to revealing the "real" truth: that he has been working for the CIA for more than 30 years, and that he had personally used the CIA's top secret "jump room" to visit Mars on several occasions as a young man. This is probably not the wildest conspiracy theory about a president that's ever circulated, but it's certainly in the top tier.

However, there's at least one witness who claims to have known the future president in his Mars-hopping days: a Seattle attorney named Andrew Basiago, who also only claims to have been to Mars himself as an Earth ambassador to a Martian civilization in the early 1980s.

But by then, Basiago says, he was an old hand with the CIA: some years before, when he was only 12, he was a participant in a top secret initiative called "Project Pegasus," an elite force that used "radiant energy" principles discovered in the papers of inventor Nikola Tesla to travel through time.

Basiago claims that he traveled through time using eight different technologies as a boy, but mainly using a teleporter that consisted of two "elliptical booms" that stood eight feet tall, positioned about ten feet apart and separated by a curtain of "radiant energy." Participants would jump through the curtain and enter a "vortal tunnel" that took them through time and space. By jumping though, Basiago claims to have attended Ford's Theatre on the night Abraham Lincoln was shot more than once—often enough that on a few occasions, he saw himself, on other trips, among the crowd. Oddly, though this would imply that each "jump" took him to the same "timeline," he says that every time he attended the theatre, the events of the night came off slightly differently, as though he were going to different "timelines" on each trip.

But Lincoln's assassination wasn't the only historic event Basiago claims to have attended. In 1972, he says, he used a "plasma confinement chamber" in East Hanover, New Jersey, to travel back to 1863 to see the Gettysburg Address. Basiago even claims that photographic evidence of this exists; in the foreground of the one photograph of Lincoln at Gettysburg that exists stands a young boy in oversized men's clothes, standing casually outside of the crowd in the background. Basiago says that he is the boy.

Basiago told his story over the course of several appearances on *Coast to Coast AM*, a radio program where conspiracies, UFOs, hauntings, and other strange phenomena are discussed during late night broadcasts. The online forums on which listeners discuss the topics spoken about on the show once brought forth the story of another alleged time traveler: the story of John Titor, who began posting on the forum in 2000 and claimed to be a time traveler from 2036. Physicists tried to drill him on the mathematics and theories behind time travel, and he seemed to pass every test.

Titor claimed that he was a soldier based in Tampa who was visiting year 2000 for personal reasons—perhaps to collect old family photos that had been destroyed by his time. He even posted schematics showing the devices he used to travel in time, and many at the time became convinced that he was telling the truth.

However, the stories he told about the future of the United States failed to come to pass. In 2001, he claimed that unrest in America surrounding the 2004 presidential election would gradually build up until it became a full-on civil war, broadly defined as a war between urban and rural parts of the country eventually splitting the United States into five regions. In 2011, he claimed, he was a young teenage soldier for a group called The Fighting Diamondbacks fighting for the rural armies. But the war, he said, would end in 2015 when Russia launched a nuclear assault destroying most American cities, killing as many as half of the people in the country and creating a "new" America in which Omaha, Nebraska, served as the nation's capital. Titor said there was an upside to this: in many ways, he said, the world was better with half of the people gone.

Titor's odd story found a lot of supporters when it was first posted, and the events of September 11, 2001, convinced many people that World War III was, in fact, at hand. However, the 2004 election came and went without anything happening in the United States that could ever reasonably be called a civil war breaking out. There was still no such war going in 2008, either, by which time Titor claimed that the war would be fully raging and undeniable.

Fans of *Coast to Coast AM* are certainly not the only people who claim to have traveled through time, though, and some of the supposed time travelers have far more bona fide military credentials than Titor, who eventually disappeared from the forums. In 1935, Sir Victor Goddard, an air marshal in the Royal Air Force, claimed that he flew into a strange storm while flying his plane above an airfield in Scotland. The turbulence was so bad that he nearly crashed, and he emerged from the storm to find that the landscape beneath him now contained strange-looking aircraft in hangars that weren't there before, all attended by officers wearing blue uniforms instead of the brown ones the RAF normally used. Four years later, the RAF officially changed the uniforms from brown to blue and began using planes like the ones he had seen after the "storm."

This wasn't Goddard's only brush with the unknown. A decade later, he overheard an officer telling of a dream he'd had in which Air Marshall Goddard had died in a wreck when the plane he was flying in iced over and crashed on a beach. That night, Goddard's plane did, indeed, ice over, and an emergency landing was forced on a beach. Though the dream had ended with Goddard dead, Goddard, having had a sort of early warning, kept his cool and brought the plane safely down. The dream he overheard may very well have saved his life.

# MONSTERS ACROSS AMERICA

Dracula, Frankenstein, the Wolf Man—these are the monsters who strike fear into the hearts of children—the same ones that parents chase away and tell their kids there's no such thing as monsters. But are they wrong?

## DOVER DEMON

For two days in 1977, the town of Dover, Massachusetts, was under attack from a bizarre creature that seemed to be from another world. The first encounter with the beast—nicknamed the Dover Demon—occurred on the evening of April 21. Bill Bartlett was out for a drive with some friends when they saw something strange climbing on a stone wall. The creature appeared to be only about three feet tall but had a giant, oversize head with large, orange eyes. The rest of the body was tan and hairless with long, thin arms and legs.

Several hours later, 15-year-old John Baxter spotted the same creature scurry up a hillside. The following day, a couple reported seeing the Demon, too. When authorities asked for a description, the couple's matched the ones given by the other witnesses except for one difference: The creature the couple encountered appeared to have glowing green eyes. Despite repeated attempts to locate it, the creature was never seen again.

## MOMO

In the early 1970s, reports came flooding in of a strange creature roaming the woods near the small town of Louisiana, Missouri. Standing nearly seven feet tall, Momo (short for Missouri Monster) was completely covered in black fur with glowing orange eyes. The first major report came in July 1971 when Joan Mills and Mary Ryan claimed to have been harassed by a "half ape, half man" creature that made bizarre noises at them as they passed it on Highway 79. Even though the creature didn't make physical contact with them, both women believed it would have harmed them had it been given the chance. That seemed to be confirmed the following year when, on July 11, 1972, brothers Terry and Wally Harrison spotted a giant, hairy beast carrying a dead dog. The boys screamed, alerting family members, who caught a glimpse of the creature before it disappeared into the woods. Sightings continued for a couple of weeks, but Momo hasn't been seen since.

## LAWNDALE THUNDERBIRD

If you're ever in Lawndale, Illinois, keep an eye out for giant birds lest they sneak up on you and whisk you away. That's what almost happened in 1977 when Lawndale residents noticed two large black birds with white-banded necks and 10- to 12-foot wingspans flying overhead. The birds, though enormous, seemed harmless enough. That is, until they swooped down and one of them reportedly tried to take off with ten-year-old Marlon Lowe while he played in his yard. The boy was not seriously injured, but the thunderbird did manage to lift the terrified boy several feet off the ground and carry him for nearly 40 feet before dropping him. Over the next few weeks, the birds were seen flying over various houses and fields in nearby towns, but, thankfully, they did not attack anyone else. And though they appear to have left Lawndale for good, reports of thunderbird sightings continue across the United States. The most recent one was on September 25, 2001, in South Greensburg, Pennsylvania.

## OHIO BRIDGE TROLLS

In May 1955, a man driving along the Miami River near Loveland, Ohio, came across a frightening sight. Huddled under a darkened bridge were several bald-headed creatures, each three to four feet tall. Spellbound, the man pulled over and watched the creatures, which he said had webbed hands and feet. Though they made no sound, the man said the creatures appeared to be communicating with each other and did not notice him watching them. However, when one of the creatures held up a wand or rod that began emitting showers of sparks, the man quickly left. He drove straight to the local police station, which dispatched a car to the bridge. A search of the area turned up nothing, and, to this day, there have been no more reported sightings of these strange creatures.

## GATORMEN

The swamplands of Florida are filled with alligators, but most of them don't have human faces. Since the 1700s, tales of strange half-man, half-alligator creatures have circulated throughout the area. Gatormen are described as having the face, neck, chest, and arms of a man and the midsection, back legs, and tail of an alligator. Unlike most other monsters and strange beasts, Gatormen reportedly prefer to travel and hunt in packs and even appear to have their own verbal language. What's more, recent sightings have them traveling outside the state of Florida and taking up residence in the swamplands of Louisiana and swimming around a remote Texas swamp in 2001.

## SKUNK APE

Since the 1960s, a creature has been spotted in the Florida Everglades that many call Bigfoot's stinky cousin: the skunk ape. The beast is said to closely resemble Bigfoot with one minor difference—it smells like rotten eggs. In late 2000, Sarasota police received an anonymous letter from a woman who complained that an escaped animal was roaming near her home at night. Included with the letter were two close-up photographs of the creature—a large beast that resembled an orangutan standing behind some palmetto leaves, baring its teeth.

## LIZARD MAN

At around 2:00 A.M. on June 29, 1988, Christopher Davis got a flat tire on a back road near the Scape Ore Swamp in South Carolina. Just as the teen finished changing the tire, a seven-foot-tall creature with scaly green skin and glowing red eyes suddenly attacked him. Davis was able to get back into his car and drive away but not before the Lizard Man managed to climb onto the roof and claw at it, trying to get inside. As he drove, Davis could see the creature had three claws on each of its "hands." Eventually, the creature fell from the car and Davis was able to escape. A search of the scene later that day turned up nothing. Despite numerous subsequent sightings, the creature has yet to be apprehended.

## DEVIL MONKEYS

Far and away, some of the strangest creatures said to be roaming the countryside are the Devil Monkeys. Take an adult kangaroo, stick a monkey or baboon head on top, and you've got yourself a Devil Monkey. By most accounts, these creatures can cover hundreds of feet in just a few quick hops. They're nothing to tangle with, either. Although Devil Monkeys have traditionally stuck to attacking livestock and the occasional family pet, some reports have them attempting to claw their way into people's homes. Originally spotted in Virginia in the 1950s, Devil Monkeys have now been spotted all across the United States. On a related note, in May 2001, residents of New Delhi, India, were sent into a panic when a four-foot-tall half-monkey, half-human creature began attacking them as they slept.

## MARYLAND'S GOATMAN

Think goats are cute and fuzzy little creatures? If so, a trip through Prince George's County in Maryland just might change your mind. Since the 1950s, people have reported horrifying encounters with a creature known only as the Goatman. From afar, many claim to have mistaken the Goatman for a human being. But as he draws nearer, his cloven feet become visible, as do the horns growing out of his head. If that's not enough to make you turn and run, reports as recent as 2006 state that the Goatman now carries an ax with him.

# LEGENDARY LAKE MILLS

Along the interstate between Madison and Milwaukee, Wisconsin, is the small town that dubbed itself "Legendary Lake Mills." It's legendary, indeed, and controversial too.

## AN UNDERWATER MYSTERY

Since the 1840s, locals have buzzed about "stone tepees" standing at the bottom of Rock Lake. The idea seems plausible. Less than three miles due east is Aztalan State Park, an archeological site where the ancient remains of a Middle-Mississippian village, temple mounds, and ceremonial complex have been restored.

But Native American legend and local folklore, combined with years of third-party research, have not been enough to persuade top scientists that there are pyramids beneath Rock Lake's waters. In fact, the phenomena has been dubbed "North America's most controversial underwater archeological discovery of the 20th century."

One theory holds that ancient Aztecs believed that their ancestors hailed from a land far north of Mexico, called Aztalan. The legend goes that in 1066, the Aztalans of Lake Mills appealed to the gods for relief from a long drought by building sacrificial pyramids. Rain came down, creating a beautiful lake and submerging the pyramids. They named the lake Tyranena, meaning "sparkling waters."

Fast-forward 800 years. When the first white settlers set up camp along Tyranena's banks in the 1830s, the resident Winnebago people shared the story of Tyranena with them. But even the Winnebago didn't quite understand the story, as it came from a "foreign tribe." The lore remained as elusive as the small islands that settlers reported as floating above the water.

Soon after the settlers arrived, a sawmill and a gristmill were built on the lake's edge, subsequently raising the water level. What little was left to see of the supposed pyramids was submerged.

## DOUBT AND CIRCUMSTANCE

Over the next 200 years, the lake would be caught up in a continuous cycle of sensationalism and doubt, false starts, and circumstance. In the early 1900s, two brothers, Claude and Lee Wilson, went out duck hunting one hot, clear day during a drought and were able to reach down and touch the so-called pyramid's apex with an oar. Local residents would find the pyramid again the next day, but by the time a reporter got onto the lake a week later, rain had fallen, ending the drought and raising the water level. Through the decades, anglers would declare their belief in the structures when they snagged their lines and nets, but interest waned.

The lore was rekindled in the 1930s when a local schoolteacher, Victor Taylor, took it upon himself to canvass residents and dive over the pyramids, without diving equipment. He described four conical underwater structures. With this "evidence," state and national agencies threw money into the effort, even hiring professional divers to explore the underwater structures. But these divers were literally mired by the lake's deteriorating, muddy bottom, mucking up belief in the pyramids once again.

Eventually the controversy would reach an MIT engineer, Max Nohl, the man who invented the first scuba-type device. A master excavator, Nohl made it his personal mission to uncover the truth beneath the lake. He rekindled the town's pyramid fever with his extensive dives and written accounts with detailed measurements.

## DEBUNKED?

While Nohl successfully made his case, the curious fact remained that no professional archeologist wanted to be associated with Rock Lake. The establishment theory contends that the lake bottom anomalies are merely glacial castoffs from the last Ice Age. In an article in the September 1962 issue of *The Wisconsin Archeologist*, the pyramids were wholly debunked by the state's academes, who alleged that Native Americans didn't work in stone and that mound-building only began 2,000 years prior, whereas Rock Lake was at least 10,000 years old. Case closed. Or not.

In July 1967, Jack Kennedy, a professional diver from Illinois, was sport diving with friends on Rock Lake. Near the end of the day, after all of his comrades had run out of air, Kennedy took one last dive...over a pyramid. Shocked at his discovery, he removed three rocks from its wall. Further analysis revealed the rocks were made of quartzite from a riverbed. The first concrete evidence was now in hand.

Kennedy continued to dive at Rock Lake, eventually making a sketch of a structure 70 feet long, 30 feet wide, and 15 feet tall, which appeared in *Skin Diver* magazine. His discovery led to a resurgence in the exploration of Rock Lake, a summer haven for leisure boaters and beachgoers. Explorers have documented stone rings, tombs, curiously long rock bars, and pyramidal structures in dives, sonic sonar, and aerial photography. In 1998, two Rock Lake enthusiasts, Archie Eschborn and Jack LeTourneau, formed Rock Lake Research Society to "document and help preserve these archeological treasures that could rewrite North American history...and persuade state officials to declare Rock Lake a historical site."

## HISTORY STILL UNWRITTEN

Does the Aztalan connection hold water? How does glacial activity fit in the picture?

To date, Rock Lake remains just that, a lake, which is still unprotected as a historical site. But locals continue to believe, if not for the archeological and anthropological truth, then for the opportunities the lore and legend provide. In Lake Mills, you can stay at the Pyramid Motel or throw back a Stone Tepee Pale Ale, made by the city's resident Tyranena Brewing Company. Or perhaps you can head to one of the city's three beaches and try your hand at uncovering the mysteries of the "sparkling waters" yourself.

# THE CHAMPION OF AMERICAN LAKE MONSTERS

In 1609, French explorer Samuel de Champlain was astonished to see a thick, eight- to ten-foot-tall creature in the waters between present-day Vermont and New York. His subsequent report set in motion the legend of Champ, the "monster" in Lake Champlain.

## EERIE ENCOUNTERS

Even before Champlain's visit, Champ was known to Native Americans as Chaousarou. Over time, Champ has become one of North America's most famous lake monsters. News stories of its existence were frequent enough that in 1873, showman P. T. Barnum offered $50,000 for the creature, dead or alive. That same year, Champ almost sank a steamboat, and in the 1880s, a number of people, including a sheriff, glimpsed it splashing playfully offshore. It is generally described as dark in color (olive green, gray, or brown) with a serpentlike body.

Sightings have continued into modern times, and witnesses have compiled some film evidence that is difficult to ignore. In 1977, a woman named Sandra Mansi photographed a long-necked creature poking its head out of the water near St. Albans, Vermont, close to the Canadian border. She estimated the animal was 10 to 15 feet long and told an investigator that its skin looked "slimy" and similar to that of an eel. Mansi presented her photo and story at a 1981 conference held at Lake Champlain. Although she had misplaced the negative by then, subsequent analyses of the photo have generally failed to find any evidence that it was manipulated.

In September 2002, a researcher named Dennis Hall, who headed a lake monster investigation group known as Champ Quest, videotaped what looked like three creatures undulating through the water near Ferrisburgh, Vermont. Hall claimed that he saw unidentifiable animals in Lake Champlain on 19 separate occasions.

In 2006, two fishermen captured digital video footage of what appeared to be parts of a very large animal swimming in the lake. The images were thoroughly examined under the direction of ABC News technicians, and though the creature on the video could not be proved to be Champ, the team could find nothing to disprove it, either.

## CHAMP OR CHUMP?

As the sixth-largest freshwater lake in the United States (and stretching about six miles into Quebec, Canada), Lake Champlain provides ample habitat and nourishment for a good-size water cryptic, or unknown animal. The lake plunges as deep as 400 feet in spots and covers 490 square miles.

Skeptics offer the usual explanations for Champ sightings: large sturgeons, floating logs or water plants, otters, or an optical illusion caused by sunlight and shadow. Others think Champ could be a remnant of a species of primitive whale called a zeuglodon or an ancient marine reptile known as a plesiosaur, both believed by biologists to be long extinct. But until uncontestable images of the creature's entire body are produced, this argument will undoubtedly continue.

Champ does claim one rare, official nod to the probability of its existence: Legislation by both the states of New York and Vermont proclaim that Champ is a protected—though unknown—species and make it illegal to harm the creature in any way.

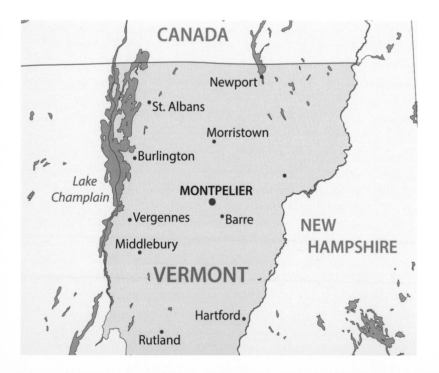

# THE MYSTERY OF CROP CIRCLES

The result of cyclonic winds? Attempted alien communication? Evidence of hungry cows with serious OCD? There are many theories as to how crop circles, or grain stalks flattened in recognizable patterns, have come to exist. Most people dismiss them as pranks, but there are more than a few who believe there's something otherworldly going on.

## YE OLE CROP CIRCLE

Some experts believe the first crop circles date back to the late 1600s, but there isn't much evidence to support them. Other experts cite evidence of more than 400 simple circles 6 to 20 feet in diameter that appeared worldwide hundreds of years ago. The kinds of circles they refer to are still being found today, usually after huge, cyclonic thunderstorms pass over a large expanse of agricultural land. These circles are much smaller and not nearly as precise as the geometric, mathematically complex circles that started cropping up in the second half of the 20th century. Still, drawings and writings about these smaller circles lend weight to the claims of believers that the crop circle phenomenon isn't a new thing.

The International Crop Circle Database reports stories of "UFO nests" in British papers during the 1960s. About a decade or so later, crop circles fully captured the attention (and the imagination) of the masses.

## NO, VIRGINIA, THERE AREN'T ANY ALIENS

In 1991, two men from Southampton, England, came forward with a confession. Doug Bower and Dave Chorley admitted that they were responsible for the majority of the crop circles found in England during the preceding two decades.

Inspired by stories of "UFO nests" in the 1960s, the two decided to add a little excitement to their sleepy town. With boards, string, and a few simple navigational tools, the men worked through the night to create complex patterns in fields that could be seen from the road. It worked, and before long, much of the Western world was caught up in crop circle fever. Some claimed it was irrefutable proof that UFOs were landing on Earth. Others said God was trying to communicate with humans "through the language of mathematics." For believers, there was no doubt that supernatural or extraterrestrial forces were at work. But skeptics were thrilled to hear the confession from Bower and Chorley, since they never believed the circles to be anything but a prank in the first place.

Before the men came forward, more crop circles appeared throughout the 1980s and '90s, many of them not made by Bower and Chorley. Circles "mysteriously" occurred in Australia, Canada, the United States, Argentina, India, and even Afghanistan. In 1995, more than 200 cases of crop circles were reported worldwide. In 2001, a formation that appeared in Wiltshire, England, contained 409 circles and covered more than 12 acres.

Many were baffled that anyone could believe these large and admittedly rather intricate motifs were anything but human-made. Plus, the more media coverage crop circles garnered, the more new crop circles appeared. Other people came forward, admitting that they were the "strange and unexplained power" behind the circles. Even then, die-hard believers dismissed the hoaxers, vehemently suggesting that they were either players in a government cover-up, captives of aliens forced to throw everyone off track, or just average Joes looking for 15 minutes of fame by claiming to have made something that was clearly the work of nonhumans.

Scientists were deployed to ascertain the facts. In 1999, a well-funded team of experts was assembled to examine numerous crop circles in the UK. The verdict? Beyond a shadow of a doubt, humans created at least 80 percent of the circles. Footprints, abandoned tools, and video of a group of hoaxers caught in the act all debunked the theory that crop circles were created by aliens.

## BUT STILL...

So if crop circles are nothing more than hoaxers having fun or artists playing with a unique medium, why are we still so interested? Movies such as *Signs* in 2002 capitalized on the public's fascination with the phenomenon, and crop circles still capture headlines. Skeptics will scoff, but from time to time, there is a circle that doesn't quite fit the profile of a human-made prank.

There have been claims that fully functional cell phones cease to work once the caller steps inside certain crop circles. Could it be caused by some funky ion-scramble emitted by an extraterrestrial force? Some researchers have tried to recreate the circles and succeeded, but only with the use of high-tech tools and equipment that wouldn't be available to the average prankster. If humans made all of these circles, why are so few people busted for trespassing in the middle of the night? And where are all the footprints?

Eyewitness accounts of UFOs rising from fields can hardly be considered irrefutable evidence, but there are several reports from folks who swear they saw ships, lights, and movement in the sky just before crop circles were discovered.

# MYSTERIOUS DISAPPEARANCES IN THE BERMUDA TRIANGLE

The Bermuda Triangle is an infamous stretch of the Atlantic Ocean bordered by Florida, Bermuda, and Puerto Rico where strange disappearances have occurred throughout history. The coast guard doesn't recognize the Triangle or the supernatural explanations for the mysterious disappearances. There are some probable causes for the missing vessels—hurricanes, undersea earthquakes, and magnetic fields that interfere with compasses and other positioning devices. But it's much more interesting to think they were sucked into another dimension, abducted by aliens, or simply vanished into thin air.

## FLIGHT 19

On the afternoon of December 5, 1945, five Avenger torpedo bombers left the Naval Air Station at Fort Lauderdale, Florida, with Lt. Charles Taylor in command of a crew of 13 student pilots. About 90 minutes into the flight, Taylor radioed the base to say that his compasses weren't working, but he figured he was somewhere over the Florida Keys. The lieutenant who received the signal told Taylor to fly north toward Miami, as long as he was sure he was actually over the Keys. Although he was an experienced pilot, Taylor got horribly turned around, and the more he tried to get out of the Keys, the further out to sea he and his crew traveled. As night fell, radio signals worsened, until, finally, there was nothing at all from Flight 19. A U.S. Navy investigation reported that Taylor's confusion caused the disaster, but his mother convinced them to change the official report to read that the planes went down for "causes unknown." The planes have never been recovered.

## THE SPRAY

Joshua Slocum, the first man to sail solo around the world, never should have been lost at sea, but it appears that's exactly what happened. In 1909, the *Spray* left the East Coast of the United States for Venezuela via the Caribbean Sea. Slocum was never heard from or seen again and was declared dead in 1924. The ship was solid, and Slocum was a pro, so nobody knows what happened. Perhaps a larger ship felled him or maybe pirates took him down. No one knows for sure that Slocum disappeared within the Triangle's waters, but Bermuda buffs claim Slocum's story as part of the area's mysterious and supernatural legacy.

## USS CYCLOPS

As World War I heated up, America went to battle. In 1918, the USS *Cyclops*, commanded by Lt. G. W. Worley, was sent to Brazil to refuel Allied ships. With 309 people onboard, the ship left Rio de Janeiro in February and reached Barbados in March. After that, the *Cyclops* was never seen or heard from again. The navy says in its official statement, "The disappearance of this ship has been one of the most baffling mysteries in the annals of the navy, all attempts to locate her having proved unsuccessful. There were no enemy submarines in the western Atlantic at that time, and in December 1918, every effort was made to obtain from German sources information regarding the disappearance of the vessel."

## STAR TIGER

The *Star Tiger*, commanded by Capt. B. W. McMillan, was flying from England to Bermuda in early 1948. On January 30, McMillan said he expected to arrive in Bermuda at 5:00 A.M., but neither he nor any of the 31 people onboard the *Star Tiger* were ever heard from again. When the Civil Air Ministry launched an investigation, they learned that the S.S. *Troubadour* had reported seeing a low-flying aircraft halfway between Bermuda and the entrance to Delaware Bay. If that aircraft was the *Star Tiger*, it was drastically off course. According to the Civil Air Ministry, the fate of the *Star Tiger* remains unknown.

## STAR ARIEL

On January 17, 1949, a Tudor IV aircraft like the *Star Tiger* left Bermuda with seven crewmembers and 13 passengers en route to Jamaica. That morning, Capt. J. C. McPhee reported that the flight was going smoothly. Shortly afterward, another more cryptic message came from the captain, when he reported that he was changing his frequency, and then nothing more was heard—ever. More than 60 aircraft and 13,000 people were deployed to look for the *Star Ariel*, but no hint of debris or wreckage was ever found. After the *Star Ariel* disappeared, production of Tudor IVs ceased.

## FLIGHT 201

This Cessna left for Fort Lauderdale on March 31, 1984, en route for Bimini Island in the Bahamas, but it never made it. Not quite midway to its destination, the plane slowed its airspeed significantly, but no distress signals came from the plane. Suddenly, the plane dropped from the air into the water, completely vanishing from the radar. A woman on Bimini Island swore she saw a plane plunge into the sea about a mile offshore, but no wreckage has ever been found.

## TEIGNMOUTH ELECTRON

Who said that the Bermuda Triangle only swallows up ships and planes? Who's to say it can't also make a man go mad? Perhaps that's what happened on the *Teignmouth Electron* in 1969. *The Sunday Times* Golden Globe race of 1968 left England on October 31 and required each contestant to sail his ship solo. Donald Crowhurst was one of the entrants, but he never made it to the finish line. The *Electron* was found abandoned in the middle of the Bermuda Triangle in July 1969. Logbooks recovered from the ship reveal that Crowhurst was deceiving organizers about his position in the race and going a little bit nutty out there in the big blue ocean. The last entry of his log was dated June 29—it is believed that Crowhurst jumped overboard and drowned himself in the Triangle.

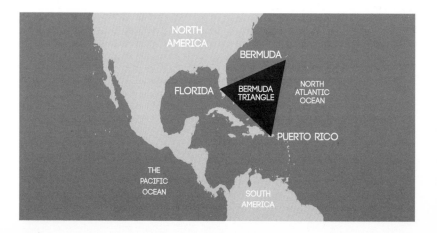

# GHOST LIGHTS

The legends are similar, no matter the locale. It's whispered that mysterious lights that blink and wink in the night are the spirits of long-dead railroad workers, jealous and jilted lovers, or lost children. They go by many names: marsh lights, ghost lights, will-o'-the-wisp, feu follet, earth lights, and even, to the skeptical, swamp gas. They occur in remote areas, often near old railway tracks or power transmitters. Some are thought to issue from the geomagnetic fields of certain kinds of rock. But tales of lights that change color, follow people, foil electrical systems, or perform acrobatic stunts are harder to explain.

## MYSTERIOUS MARFA LIGHTS

The famed Marfa Lights of Marfa, Texas, have become almost synonymous with the term ghost lights. Since 1883, they have been spotted in an area southwest of the Chisos Mountains, some 200 miles south of El Paso. The lights appear almost playful in their gyrations, skimming over the fields, bobbing like a yo-yo, or chasing visitors. One woman reportedly witnessed a white ball of light three feet in diameter that bounced in slow motion alongside her car as she drove through the Chisos one night. Some of the lights have been attributed to auto headlights miles away across the desert, but the Marfa Lights were witnessed long before automobiles came to the area.

## THE PECULIAR PAULDING LIGHT

According to legend, an old railway brakeman was killed near the Choate Branch Railroad tracks that used to run near Paulding, Michigan, along the northern Wisconsin–Michigan border. People have observed strange lights near the tracks for decades, and it is said that they're from the railman's ghostly lantern swinging as he walks his old beat. Others, armed with telescopes and binoculars, believe that the famed Paulding Light is actually caused by headlights shining from a highway a few miles away.

Still, many claim that the lights behave like anything but distant reflections. The lights are said to change from red to green, zoom up close as if peering into people's cars, chase people, flash through automobiles either cutting off all electric power or turning radios off and on, and zigzag through the nearby woods. Crowds flock to the Robins Wood Road site off Highway 45 to see the phenomenon for themselves, and a wooden sign has been erected complete with a drawing of a ghost swinging a lantern.

## THE FIERY FEU FOLLET

During the mid-18th century, when Detroit was being settled by the French, aristocrats and working folks feared the *feu follet*—spirit lights of the marshy river area. One local legend tells of a rich landowner who nearly drowned one stormy night when the brilliant lights lured him into a swamp. Luckily, two guests staying at his house heard his terrified cries and managed to rescue him. At the time, the prevailing theory of the marsh lights was that windows had to be closed when the feu follet were near or they would enter the house, snake their way into the windpipes of those present, and choke them to death.

## BAFFLING BROWN MOUNTAIN LIGHTS

Although scoffed at as nothing more than reflected train lights, the multicolored light show in the foothills of North Carolina's Blue Ridge Mountains has fascinated humans since an early explorer reported it in 1771, and even earlier according to Native American legend. Several centuries ago, many people were killed during a battle between the Cherokee and the Catawba tribes. Legend has it that the Brown Mountain Lights are the spirits of those lost warriors.

Another tale states that a plantation owner got lost hunting on Brown Mountain and that one of his slaves came looking for him, swinging a lantern to light his way. The slave never found his owner but still walks the mountainside with his eternal lantern. Still another legend claims the lights come from the spirit of a woman murdered on the mountain by her husband in 1850.

Whatever the source of the colorful lights, they come in many shapes, from glowing orbs to trailing bursts to still, white areas. Crowds flock to at least three locations to view the lights, but one of the most popular is the Brown Mountain overlook on Highway 181, 20 miles north of Morganton.

# UNEXPLAINED PHENOMENA

If a phenomenon can't be readily explained, does that make it any less true to those who witnessed it?

## THE PHILADELPHIA EXPERIMENT

The Philadelphia Experiment (aka Project Rainbow) is one for the "too strange not to be true" file. Allegedly, on October 28, 1943, a super-secret experiment was being conducted at the Philadelphia Naval Shipyard. Its objective? To make the USS *Eldridge* and all of its inhabitants disappear! That day, some reported that the *Eldridge* became almost entirely invisible amidst a flash of blue light. Inexplicably, it had not only vanished but also tele-transported—at the same instant, it was witnessed some 375 miles away at the U.S. Naval Base in Norfolk, Virginia. Legend has it that most sailors involved in the experiment became violently ill afterward. They were the lucky ones. Others were supposedly fused to the ship's deck or completely vaporized and were never seen again. Justifiably horrified by these results, the navy is said to have pulled the plug on future experiments and employed brainwashing techniques to help the affected seamen forget what happened.

## MOODUS NOISES

The Moodus Noises are thunder-like sounds that emanate from caves near East Haddam, Connecticut, where the Salmon and Moodus Rivers meet. The name itself is derived from the Native American word *machemoodus*, which means "place of noises." When European settlers filtered into the area in the late 1600s, the Wangunk tribe warned them about the odd, supernatural sounds. Whether or not anything otherworldly exists there is open to debate. In 1979, seismologists showed that the noises were always accompanied by small earthquakes (some measuring as low as magnitude 2 on the Richter scale) spread over a small area some 5,000 feet deep by 800 feet wide. But this doesn't explain the fact that no known fault line exists at Moodus. Nor does it describe how small tremors—producing 100 times less ground motion than is detectable by human beings—can generate big, bellowing booms. The mystery and the booms continue.

## ROCK CONCERT

Visitors looking to entertain themselves at Pennsylvania's Ringing Rocks Park often show up toting hammers. Seems odd, but they're necessary for the proper tone. Ringing

Rocks is a seven-acre boulder field that runs about ten feet deep. For reasons that are still unexplained, some of these rocks ring like bells when struck lightly by a hammer or other object. Because igneous diabase rocks don't usually do this, the boulder field has caused quite a stir through the years. In 1890, Dr. J. J. Ott held what may have been the world's first "rock concert" at the park. He assembled rocks of different pitches, enlisted the aid of a brass band for accompaniment, and went to town.

## CRY ME A RED RIVER

Tales of "crying" statues have become almost commonplace. Sometimes they're revealed as hoaxes, but other times they can truly confound the senses. The Mother Mary statue that cries "tears of blood" at the Vietnamese Catholic Martyrs Church in Sacramento apparently began crying in November 2005 when parishioners discovered a dark reddish substance flowing from her left eye. A priest wiped it away only to see it miraculously reappear a moment later. News of the incident spread like…well, like news of a crying Mother Mary statue. Soon, hordes of the faithful made a pilgrimage to witness the miracle. Skeptics say that black paint used as eyeliner on the statue is the true culprit and that her "tears" are closer to this color than red. The faithful think the nonbelievers are blinded by anything but the light because the tears continually reappear even after the excess substance is wiped away.

# ARE YOU GOING TO EAT THAT JESUS?

Images of religious icons, particularly Jesus and the Virgin Mary, sometimes show up in the oddest places. Some people believe they are divine. What's the story?

Sightings of religious symbols or images, called religious simulacra, in unexpected places are common enough that they've become incorporated into pop culture. Many of the people who discover or are involved in these sightings consider them to be miraculous events. Some also claim that the objects in which the images appear have special properties, such as bringing good luck or being immune to the ravages of time.

## JESUS AND MARY

For Christians, Jesus and the Virgin Mary are among the most significant religious figures, and not coincidentally, they also seem to make the most common appearances—often in food. Perhaps the quintessential sighting of a Christian religious symbol in food occurred in 1978, when a New Mexico woman named Maria Rubio was making a burrito. She noticed that a burn on the tortilla appeared to be in the shape of Jesus' head. After receiving the blessing of a priest, she built a shrine to house the tortilla and even quit her job to tend to the shrine full-time.

## SELLING SIMULACRA

Sightings of religious images can have commercial as well as spiritual implications. In 1996, someone at a coffee shop in Nashville, Tennessee, discovered a cinnamon bun that bore a striking resemblance to Mother Teresa. The coffee shop parlayed the discovery into a line of merchandise, including coffee mugs and T-shirts. The merchandise was marketed with a NunBun trademark after Mother Teresa asked the shop to stop using the phrase "Immaculate Confection."

The proliferation of Internet auction sites such as eBay has created a market for these "miraculous" objects. One of the widest-known auctions occurred in 2004, when a Florida woman named Diane Duyser auctioned part of a grilled cheese sandwich she claimed bore the image of the Virgin Mary on eBay. Duyser asserted that the sandwich, which she had been storing since it was made in 1994, had never grown moldy and had brought her good luck, allowing her to win $70,000 at a casino. The sandwich was eventually purchased by another casino for $28,000.

Religious sightings—especially if they have been contrived somehow—are not always viewed in a positive light. In 1997, Nike produced several models of basketball shoes that unintentionally featured a logo that, when viewed from right to left, resembled the Arabic word for Allah. The Council on American-Islamic Relations (CAIR) quickly demanded an apology, and Nike had little choice but to recall the shoes. The settlement between Nike and CAIR also included Arabic training for Nike graphic designers and Nike-built playgrounds in Muslim communities.

## A SCIENTIFIC EXPLANATION?

While the parties involved in sightings of religious symbols often consider them to be miraculous in nature, the prevailing scientific view is that, rather than miraculous, they are occurrences of pareidolia, a psychological phenomenon in which random stimuli are interpreted as being meaningful in some way. As part of its intellectual process, the mind tries to make sense of what may be unrelated images. This is the same phenomenon that psychologists credit with forming the likeness of a man in the moon or shapes in clouds. It's also what's involved when the brain creates pictures from the famous Rorschach inkblots.

# A FIERY DEBATE: SPONTANEOUS HUMAN COMBUSTION

Proponents contend that the phenomenon—in which a person suddenly bursts into flames—is very real. Skeptics, however, are quick to explain it away.

## THE CURIOUS CASE OF HELEN CONWAY

A photo documents the gruesome death of Helen Conway. Visible in the black-and-white image—taken in 1964 in Delaware County, Pennsylvania—is an oily smear that was her torso and, behind, an ashen specter of the upholstered bedroom chair she occupied. The picture's most haunting feature might be her legs, thin and ghostly pale, clearly intact and seemingly unscathed by whatever it was that consumed the rest of her.

What consumed her, say proponents of a theory that people can catch fire without an external source of ignition, was spontaneous human combustion. It's a classic case, believers assert: Conway was immolated by an intense, precisely localized source of heat that damaged little else in the room. Adding to the mystery, the investigating fire marshal said that it took just twenty-one minutes for her to burn away and that he could not identify an outside accelerant.

If Conway's body ignited from within and burned so quickly she had no time to rise and seek help, hers wouldn't be the first or last death to fit the pattern of spontaneous human combustion.

The phenomenon was documented as early as 1763 by Frenchman Jonas Dupont in his collection of accounts, published as *De Incendis Corporis Humani Spontaneis*. Charles Dickens's 1852 novel *Bleak House* sensationalized the issue with the spontaneous-combustion death of a character named Krook. That humans have been reduced to ashes with little damage to their surroundings is not the stuff of fiction, however. Many documented cases exist. The question is, did these people combust spontaneously?

## HOW IT HAPPENS

Theories advancing the concept abound. Early hypotheses held that victims, such as Dickens's Krook, were likely alcoholics so besotted that their very flesh became flammable. Later conjecture blamed the influence of geomagnetism. A 1996 book by John Heymer, *The Entrancing Flame*, maintained emotional distress could lead to explosions of defective mitochondria. These outbursts cause cellular releases of hydrogen and oxygen and trigger crematory reactions in the body. That same year, Larry E. Arnold— publicity material calls him a Parascientist—published *Ablaze! The Mysterious Fires of Spontaneous Human Combustion*. Arnold claimed sufferers were struck by a subatomic particle he had discovered and named the "pyrotron."

Perhaps somewhat more credible reasoning came out of Brooklyn, New York, where the eponymous founder of Robin Beach Engineers Associated (described as a scientific detective agency) linked the theory of spontaneous human combustion with proven instances of individuals whose biology caused them to retain intense concentrations of static electricity.

## A CONTROVERSY IS SPARKED

Skeptics are legion. They suspect that accounts are often embellished or important facts are ignored. That the unfortunate Helen Conway was overweight and a heavy smoker, for instance, likely played a key role in her demise.

Indeed, Conway's case is considered by some to be evidence of the wick effect, which might be today's most forensically respected explanation for spontaneous human combustion. It holds that an external source, such as a dropped cigarette, ignites bedding, clothing, or furnishings. This material acts like an absorbing wick, while the body's fat takes on the fueling role of candle wax. The burning fat liquefies, saturating the bedding, clothing, or furnishings, and keeps the heat localized.

The result is a long, slow immolation that burns away fatty tissues, organs, and associated bone, leaving leaner areas, such as legs, untouched. Experiments on pig carcasses show it can take five or more hours, with the body's water boiling off ahead of the spreading fire.

Under the wick theory, victims are likely to already be unconscious when the fire starts. They're in closed spaces with little moving air, so the flames are allowed to smolder, doing their work without disrupting the surroundings or alerting passersby.

Nevertheless, even the wick effect theory, like all other explanations of spontaneous human combustion, has scientific weaknesses. The fact remains, according to the mainstream science community, that evidence of spontaneous human combustion is entirely circumstantial, and that not a single proven eyewitness account exists to substantiate anyone's claims of "Poof—the body just went up in flames!"

# WEIRD WEATHER

We've all heard that neither rain, snow, sleet nor hail, will stop our determined mail carriers, but how about a few rounds of ball lightning or tiny frogs dropping from the sky? Apparently, Mother Nature has a sense of humor. Here are some of the weirdest weather phenomena encountered on Planet Earth.

## GREAT BALLS OF LIGHTNING

In 1962, a Long Island couple was astounded to see a fiery, basketball-size orb roll into their living room through an open window. The fireball passed between the pair, continued through the room, and disappeared down an adjacent hallway. Exactly how lightning or any other electrical anomaly can form itself into a ball and zigzag at different speeds is not well understood.

## OTHERWORLDLY LIGHTS: ST. ELMO'S FIRE

A weird haze of light glimmering around a church steeple during a storm, a rosy halo over someone's head, or a ghostly light swirling around the mast of a wave-tossed ship—these are all possible manifestations of the strange, bluish-white light known as St. Elmo's Fire, which may be a signal that a lightning strike to the glowing area is imminent. The light is a visible, electric discharge produced by heavy storms. It was named after St. Erasmus, aka St. Elmo, the patron saint of sailors.

## WHEN THE MOON GETS THE BLUES

Everyone understands that the phrase "once in a blue moon" refers to a very unusual occurrence, since blue moons are rare. But a blue moon is not actually blue. In fact, a blue moon is determined by the calendar, not by its color. Typically, there is one full moon per month, but occasionally, a second full moon will sneak into a monthly cycle. When this happens, the second full moon is referred to as a "blue moon," which happens every two to three years. But at times, the moon has been known to appear blue, or even green, often after a volcanic eruption leaves tiny ash and dust particles in the earth's atmosphere.

## GREEN FLASH: WHEN THE SUN GOES GREEN

The term *green flash* may sound like a comic book superhero, but it is actually a strange flash of green light that appears just before the setting sun sinks into the horizon. Some have suggested that rare fluctuations in solar winds may be responsible for green glows and flashes that sometimes appear in the atmosphere just before sunset. Some believe it's just a mirage. But others contend that a green flash occurs when layers of the earth's atmosphere act like a prism. Whatever causes the emerald hue, seeing a flash of green light along the horizon can be an eerie and unsettling experience.

## LAVA LAMPS IN THE SKY: AURORA BOREALIS

Like a neon sign loosened from its tubing, the aurora borealis sends multicolored arches, bands, and streams of luminous beauty throughout the northern skies whenever solar flares are at their height. This occurs when electrons ejected from the sun's surface hit Earth's atmospheric particles and charge them until they glow. The electrons are attracted to Earth's magnetic poles, which is why they are seen mainly in the far northern or southern latitudes. In the southern hemisphere, they are called *aurora australis*. *Aurora polaris* refers to the lights of either pole.

## IT'S RAINING FROGS!

Startling as the thought of being pelted from above by buckets of hapless amphibians may be, reports of the sky raining frogs have occurred for so long that the problem was even addressed in the first century A.D., when a Roman scholar, Pliny the Elder, theorized that frog "seeds" were already present in the soil. *Scientific American* reported a frog fall over Kansas City, Missouri, in July 1873, in numbers so thick they "darkened the air." No one knows for certain why this happens, but one theory is that the small animals—fish, birds, and lizards are also common—are carried from other locations by tornadoes or waterspouts.

## SPOUTING OFF

Ancient people feared waterspouts and understandably so. Waterspouts are actually tornadoes that form over a body of water, whirling at speeds as fast as 190 miles per hour. Waterspouts start with parent clouds that pull air near the surface into a vortex at an increasing rate, until water is pulled up toward the cloud. One of the world's top waterspout hot spots is the Florida Keys, which may see as many as 500 per year. They can also occur in relatively calm areas such as Lake Tahoe, on the California-Nevada border. There, a Native American legend said that waterspouts, which they called "waterbabies," appeared at the passing of great chiefs to take them to heaven.

## MIRAGES: OPTICAL CONFUSION

Mirages have been blamed for everything from imaginary

waterholes in deserts to sightings of the Loch Ness Monster. They come in two forms: hallucinations or environmental illusions based on tricks of light, shadow, and atmosphere. In April 1977, residents of Grand Haven, Michigan, were able to plainly see the shimmering lights of Milwaukee, Wisconsin, some 75 miles across Lake Michigan.
The sighting was confirmed by the flashing pattern of Milwaukee's red harbor beacon. Another rare type of water mirage is the *fata morgana*, which produces a double image that makes mundane objects look gigantic and may account for some reports of sea monsters.

## COBWEBS FROM HEAVEN?

On their 40-year desert tour with Moses, the Israelites were blessed with a strange substance called manna that fell from the sky. People in other places have also witnessed falls of unknown material, often resembling cobwebs. In October 1881, great quantities of weblike material fell around the cities of Milwaukee, Green Bay, and Sheboygan, Wisconsin. Newspapers speculated that the strong, white strands had come from "gossamer spiders" due to their lightness. The same thing allegedly happened in 1898 in Montgomery, Alabama.

## DOUBLE THE RAINBOWS, DOUBLE THE GOLD?

Rainbow stories abound; ancient Irish lore promises a pot of leprechaun's gold at the end of a rainbow, and biblical tradition says God set a rainbow in the sky as a promise to Noah that Earth would never again be destroyed by water. Rainbows are formed when sunlight passes through water droplets, usually at the end of a rainstorm, and the droplets separate the light like tiny prisms into a spectrum from red to violet. A secondary rainbow, set outside the first one and in the reverse order of colors, is formed by a second set of light refractions to create the spectacular double rainbow. Conditions have to be just right to see the double rainbow because the secondary arch of colors is much paler than the primary rainbow and is not always visible.

# PHANTOM SHIPS AND GHOSTLY CREWS

Ghost ships come in a variety of shapes and sizes, but they all seem to have the ability to slip back and forth between the watery veil of this world and the next, often making appearances that foretell of impending doom. Come with us now as we set sail in search of some of the most famous ghost ships in maritime history.

## THE PALATINE

According to legend, shortly after Christmas 1738, the *Princess Augusta* ran aground and broke into pieces off the coast of Block Island, Rhode Island. Roughly 130 years later, poet John Greenleaf Whittier renamed the European vessel and told his version of the shipwreck in his poem *The Palatine*, which was published in *Atlantic Monthly*. Today, strange lights, said to be the fiery ghost ship, are still reported in the waters surrounding Block Island, especially on the Saturday between Christmas and New Year's Day.

## MARY CELESTE

*The Amazon* was cursed from the beginning. During her maiden voyage, the *Amazon*'s captain died. After being salvaged by an American company that renamed her the *Mary Celeste*, the ship left New York on November 7, 1872, bound for Genoa, Italy. Onboard were Captain Benjamin Briggs, his family, and a crew of seven.

Nearly a month later, on December 4, the crew of the *Dei Gratia* found the abandoned ship. There was plenty of food and water onboard the *Mary Celeste*, but the only living soul on the ship was a cat. The crew and the captain's family were missing, and no clues remained as to where they went.

The last entry in the captain's logbook was dated almost two weeks prior to the ship's discovery, meaning it had somehow piloted itself all that time.

To this day, the fate of the members of the *Mary Celeste* remains unknown, as does how the ship piloted its way across the ocean non-crewed for weeks. Many believe she was piloted by a ghostly crew that kept her safe until she was found.

## IRON MOUNTAIN

A ship disappearing on the high seas is one thing, but on a river? That's exactly what happened to the *Iron Mountain*. In June 1872, the 180-foot-long ship left New Orleans heading for Pittsburgh via the Mississippi River with a crew of more than 50 men. A day after picking up additional cargo, which was towed behind the ship in barges, the *Iron Mountain* steamed its way north and promptly vanished. Later that day, the barges were recovered floating in the river, but the *Iron Mountain* and its entire crew were never seen nor heard from again. For years after it disappeared, ship captains would whisper to each other about how the *Iron Mountain* was simply sucked up into another dimension through a ghostly portal.

## FLYING DUTCHMAN

Easily the world's most famous ghost ship, the story of the *Flying Dutchman* is legendary. Stories say that during the 1800s, a Dutch ship captained by Hendrick Vanderdecken was attempting to sail around the Cape of Good Hope when a violent storm came up. Rather than pull into port, the *Dutchman*'s stubborn captain claimed he would navigate around the Cape even if it took him all of eternity to do so. The ship and all of the crew were lost in the storm, and as foreshadowed by Vanderdecken, they were, indeed, condemned to sail the high seas for all eternity.

Almost immediately, people from all over the world began spotting the Dutch ship silently moving through the ocean, often cast in an eerie glow. Because of the legend associated with Captain Vanderdecken, sightings of the *Flying Dutchman* are now thought to be signs of bad things to come. Case in point: The most recent sighting of the vessel occurred off the coast of North Carolina's Outer Banks prior to Hurricane Isabel in 2003.

# THE GREENBRIER GHOST: TESTIMONY FROM THE OTHER SIDE

The strange tale of the Greenbrier Ghost stands out in the annals of ghost lore. Not only is it part of supernatural history, it is also part of the history of the U.S. judicial system. To this day, it is the only case in which a crime was solved and a murderer convicted based on the testimony of a ghost.

## A DOOMED MARRIAGE

Little is known about her life, but it is believed that Zona Heaster was born in Greenbrier County, West Virginia, around 1873. In October 1896, she met Erasmus "Edward" Stribbling Trout Shue, a drifter who had recently moved to the area to work as a blacksmith. A short time later, the two were married, despite the animosity felt toward Shue by Zona's mother, Mary Jane Heaster, who had instantly disliked him.

Unfortunately, the marriage was short-lived. In January 1897, a young neighbor boy who had come to the house on an errand discovered Zona's body at home. After he found Zona lying on the floor at the bottom of the stairs, he ran to get the local doctor and coroner, Dr. George W. Knapp. By the time Dr. Knapp arrived, Shue had come home, found his wife, and carried her body upstairs where he laid her on the bed and dressed her in her best clothing—a high-necked, stiff-collared dress with a big scarf tied around her neck and a veil placed over her face.

While Dr. Knapp was examining Zona's body in an attempt to determine the cause of death, Shue allegedly stayed by his wife's side, cradling her head, sobbing, and clearly distressed over anyone touching her body. As a result, Knapp did not do a thorough examination. Although he did notice some bruising on Zona's neck, he initially listed her cause of death as "everlasting faint" and then as "childbirth." Whether or not Zona was pregnant is unknown, but Dr. Knapp had been treating her for some time prior to her death.

When Mary Jane Heaster was informed of her daughter's death, her face grew dark as she uttered: "The devil has killed her!" Zona's body was taken to her parents' home where it was displayed for the wake.

Those who came to pay their respects whispered about Shue's erratic behavior—one minute he'd be expressing intense grief and sadness, then displaying frenetic outbursts the next. He would not allow anyone to get close to the coffin, especially when he placed a pillow and a rolled-up cloth around his wife's head to help her "rest easier." Still, when Zona's body was moved to the cemetery, several people noted a strange looseness to her head. Not surprisingly, people started to talk.

## GHOSTLY MESSAGES FROM THE OTHER SIDE

Mary Jane Heaster did not have to be convinced that Shue was acting suspiciously about Zona's death. She had always hated him and wished her daughter had never married him. She had a sneaking suspicion that something wasn't right, but she didn't know how to prove it.

After the funeral, as Heaster was folding the sheet from inside the coffin, she noticed that it had an unusual odor. When she placed it into the basin to wash it, the water turned red. Stranger still, the sheet turned pink and then the color in the water disappeared. Even after Heaster boiled the sheet, the stain remained. To her, the bizarre "bloodstains" were a sign that Zona had been murdered.

For the next four weeks, Heaster prayed fervently every night that Zona would come to her and explain the details of her death. Soon after, her prayers were answered. For four nights, Zona's spirit appeared at her mother's bedside, first as a bright light, but then the air in the room got cold and her apparition took form. She told her mother that Shue had been an abusive and cruel husband, and in a fit of rage, he had attacked her because he thought she had not cooked any meat for supper. He'd broken her neck, and as evidence, Zona's ghost spun her head around until it was facing backward.

Heaster's suspicions were correct: Shue had killed Zona and she'd come back from beyond the grave to prove it.

## OPENING THE GRAVE

After Zona's ghostly visit, Heaster tried to convince the local prosecutor, John Alfred Preston, to reopen the investigation into her daughter's death. She pleaded that an injustice was taking place and, as evidence, she told him about her encounters with Zona's spirit. Although it seems unlikely that he would reexamine the case because of the statement of a ghost, the investigation was, in fact, reopened. Preston agreed to question Dr. Knapp and a few others involved in the case. The local newspaper reported that a number of citizens were suspicious of Zona's death, and rumors were circulating throughout the community.

Dr. Knapp admitted to Preston that his examination of Zona's body was cursory at best, so it was agreed that an autopsy would be done to settle any lingering questions. They could find out how Zona really died, and, if he was innocent, ease the suspicions surrounding Shue.

The local newspaper reported that Shue "vigorously complained" about the exhumation and autopsy of his wife's body, but he was required to attend. A jury of five men gathered together in the chilly building to watch the autopsy along with officers of the court, Shue, and other witnesses.

The autopsy findings were rather damning to Shue. When the doctors concluded that Zona's neck had been broken, Shue's head dropped, and a dark expression crossed his face. "They cannot prove that I did it," he said quietly.

A March 9 report stated: "The discovery was made that the neck was broken and the windpipe mashed. On the throat were the marks of fingers indicating that she had been choken [sic]… The neck was dislocated between the first and second vertebrae. The ligaments were torn and ruptured. The windpipe had been crushed at a point in front of the neck."

Despite the fact that—aside from Zona's ghost—the evidence against Shue was circumstantial at best, he was arrested, indicted, and formally arraigned for murder. All the while, he maintained his innocence and entered a plea of "not guilty." He repeatedly told reporters that his guilt in the matter could not be proven.

While awaiting trial, details about Shue's unsavory past came to light. Zona was actually his third wife. In 1889, while he was in prison for horse theft, he was divorced from his first wife, Allie Estelline Cutlip, who claimed that Shue had frequently beaten her during their marriage. In fact, at one point, Shue allegedly beat Cutlip so severely that a group of men had to pull him off of her and throw him into an icy river.

In 1894, Shue married his second wife, Lucy Ann Tritt, who died just eight months later under mysterious circumstances. Shue left the area in the autumn of 1896 and moved to Greenbrier. When word got out that Shue was suspected of murdering Zona, stories started circulating about the circumstances behind Tritt's death, but no wrongdoing was ever proven.

Despite the fact that he was in jail, Shue seemed in good spirits. Remarking that he was done grieving for Zona, he revealed that it was his life's dream to have seven wives. Because Zona was only wife number three and he was still fairly young, he felt confident that he could achieve his goal.

## TESTIMONY FROM A GHOST

When Shue's trial began in June 1897, numerous members of the community testified against him. Of course, Heaster's testimony was the highlight of the trial. She testified as both the mother of the victim and as the first person to notice the unusual circumstances of Zona's death. Preston wanted her to come across as sane and reliable, so he did not mention the spirit encounter, which would make Heaster look irrational and was also inadmissible as evidence. Zona's testimony obviously could not be cross-examined by the defense and, therefore, was hearsay under the law.

But unfortunately for Shue, his attorney did ask Heaster about her ghostly visit. Certainly, he was trying to destroy her credibility with the jury, characterizing her "visions" as the overactive imagination of a grieving mother. He was tenacious in trying to get her to admit that she was mistaken about what she'd seen, but Heaster zealously stuck to her story. When Shue's attorney realized that she was not going to budge from her story, he dismissed her.

But by then, the damage was done. Because the defense—not the prosecution—had brought up Zona's otherworldly testimony, the judge had a difficult time ordering the jury to ignore it. Clearly, most of the townspeople believed that Heaster really had been visited by her daughter's ghost. Shue testified in his own defense, but the jury quickly found him guilty. Ten of the jury members voted for Shue to be hanged, but because they could not reach a unanimous decision, he was sentenced to life in prison.

Shue didn't carry out his sentence for long—he died in March 1900 at the West Virginia State Penitentiary in Moundsville. Until her death in 1916, Heaster told her tale to anyone who would listen, never recanting her story of her daughter's ghostly visit.

It seems that after visiting her mother to offer details of her murder, Zona was finally able to rest in peace. Although her ghost was never seen again, she did leave a historical mark on Greenbrier County, where a roadside marker still commemorates the case today. It reads:

"Interred in nearby cemetery is Zona Heaster Shue. Her death in 1897 was presumed natural until her spirit appeared to her mother to describe how her husband Edward killed her. Autopsy on the exhumed body verified the apparition's account. Edward, found guilty of murder, was sentenced to the state prison. Only known case in which testimony from ghost helped convict a murderer."

# THE SMURL INCIDENT

In the 1970s, the "Amityville Horror" story ignited a firestorm of controversy that's still debated today. The Smurl haunting is not as well known but is equally divisive.

## SPIRIT RUMBLINGS

In 1973, Jack and Janet Smurl and their daughters Dawn and Heather moved into a duplex in West Pittston, Pennsylvania. Jack's parents occupied half of the home and Jack and Janet took the other. Nothing out of the ordinary occurred during the first 18 months that they lived there, but then odd things started to happen: Water pipes leaked repeatedly, even though they had been soldered and resoldered; claw marks were found on the bathtub, sink, and woodwork; an unexplained stain appeared on the carpet; a television burst into flames; and Dawn saw people floating in her bedroom.

In 1977, Jack and Janet welcomed twin daughters Shannon and Carin to the family. By then, the home had become Spook Central: Unplugged radios played, drawers opened and closed with no assistance, toilets flushed on their own, empty porch chairs rocked back and forth, and putrid smells circulated throughout the house.

By 1985, events at the Smurl home had taken a dangerous turn. The house was always cold, and Jack's parents often heard angry voices coming from their son's side of the duplex, even though Jack and Janet weren't arguing.

In February of that year, Janet was alone in the basement doing laundry when something called her name several times. A few days later, she was alone in the kitchen when the room became frigid; suddenly, a faceless, black, human-shaped form appeared. It then walked through the wall and was witnessed by Jack's mother.

At this point, the situation became even more bizarre. On the night Heather was confirmed into the Catholic faith, Shannon was nearly killed when a large light fixture fell from the ceiling and landed on her. On another night, Janet was violently pulled off the bed as Jack lay next to her, paralyzed and unable to help his wife as a foul odor nearly suffocated him. Periodically, heavy footsteps were heard in the attic, and rapping and scratching sounds came from the walls. Not even the family dog escaped: It was repeatedly picked up and thrown around.

## "WHO YOU GONNA CALL?"

Unwilling to be terrorized out of their home, in January 1986, the Smurls contacted psychic researchers and demonologists Ed and Lorraine Warren, who confirmed that the home was haunted by four evil spirits, including a powerful demon. The Warrens theorized that the emotions generated as the older Smurl daughters entered puberty had somehow awoken a dormant demon.

The Warrens tried prayer and playing religious music, but this only angered the demon even more. It spelled out "You filthy bastard. Get out of this house" on a mirror, violently shook drawers, filled the TV set with an eerie white light, and slapped and bit Jack and Janet.

One day, Janet decided to try communicating with the demon on her own. She told it to rap once for "yes" if it was there to harm them; it rapped once. Next, the entity unleashed a new weapon: sexual assault. A red-eyed, green-gummed succubus with an old woman's face and a young woman's body raped Jack. An incubus sexually assaulted Janet, Dawn was nearly raped, and Carin fell seriously ill with a high fever. Pig noises—which supposedly signal a serious demonic infestation—emanated from the walls.

The Smurls could not escape even by leaving their home. The creature followed them on camping trips and even bothered Jack at his job, giving new meaning to the phrase "work is hell." The family appealed to the Catholic church for help but to no avail. However, a renegade clergyman named Robert F. McKenna did try to help the Smurls by performing an exorcism in the spring of 1986, but even that didn't help.

## GOING PUBLIC

Finally, in August 1986, the family went to the media with their story. The incidents continued, but the publicity drew the attention of Paul Kurtz, chairman of the Buffalo-based Committee for the Scientific Investigation of Claims of the Paranormal (CSICOP). He offered to investigate, but the Smurls turned him down, stating that they wanted to stay with the Warrens and the church. They were also concerned that CSICOP had already decided that their story was a hoax.

The Smurls did, however, contact a medium, who came to the same conclusion as the Warrens—that there were four spirits in the home: One she couldn't identify, but she said that the others were an old woman named Abigail, a murderer named Patrick, and a very strong demon.

Another exorcism was performed in the summer of 1986, and that seemed to do the trick because the incidents stopped. But just before Christmas of that year, the black form appeared again, along with the banging noises, foul odors, and other phenomena.

## SURRENDER

The Smurls finally moved out of the home in 1988; the next owner said that she never experienced any supernatural events while she lived there.

That same year, *The Haunted*, a book based on the Smurl family's experiences, was released. And in 1991, a TV movie with the same title aired.

But the controversy surrounding the alleged haunting was just beginning. In an article written for *The Skeptical Inquirer*, CSICOP's official magazine, Paul Kurtz cited financial gains from the book deal as a reason to doubt that the incidents were authentic. He also said that for years, residents in the area had complained about foul odors coming from a sewer pipe. He cited other natural explanations for some of the incidents and raised questions about Dawn Smurl's accounts of some of the events. He further claimed that the Warrens gave him a number of conflicting reasons for why he couldn't see the video and audio evidence that they said they'd compiled.

And that's where matters stand today, with the true believers in the Smurl family's account on one side and the doubters on the other. Like the Amityville incident, the Smurl haunting is likely to be debated for a long time to come.

# A VOICE FROM BEYOND THE GRAVE

After the murder of Teresita Basa in the late 1970s, another woman began to speak in Basa's voice—saying things that only Teresita could have known—to help solve the mystery of her murder.

In February 1977, firemen broke into a burning apartment on North Pine Grove Avenue in Chicago. Beneath a pile of burning clothes, they found the naked body of 47-year-old Teresita Basa, a hospital worker who was said to be a member of the Filipino aristocracy. There were bruises on her neck and a kitchen knife was embedded in her chest. Her body was in a position that caused the police to suspect that she had been raped.

However, an autopsy revealed that she hadn't been raped; in fact, she was a virgin. Police were left without a single lead: They had no suspects and no apparent motive for the brutal murder. The solution would come from the strangest of all possible sources—a voice from beyond the grave.

## "I AM TERESITA BASA"

In the nearby suburb of Evanston, shortly after Teresita's death, Remibios Chua started going into trances during which she spoke in Tagalog in a slow, clear voice that said, "I am Teresita Basa." Although Remibios had worked at the same hospital as Teresita, they worked different shifts, and the only time they are known to have even crossed paths was during a new-employee orientation. Remibios's husband, Dr. Jose Chua, had never heard of Basa.

While speaking in Teresita's voice, Remibios's accent changed, and when she awoke from the trances, she remembered very little, if anything, about what she had said. However, while speaking in the mysterious voice, she claimed that Teresita's killer was Allan Showery, an employee at the hospital where both women had worked. She also stated that he had killed her while stealing jewelry for rent money.

Through Remibios's lips, the voice pleaded for them to contact the police. The frightened couple initially resisted, fearing that the authorities would think that they should be locked away. But when the voice returned and continued pleading for an investigation, the Chuas finally contacted the Evanston police, who put them in touch with Joe Stachula, a criminal investigator for the Chicago Police Department.

Lacking any other clues, Stachula interviewed the Chuas. During their conversation, Remibios not only named the killer, but she also told Stachula exactly where to find the jewelry that Showery had allegedly stolen from Teresita. Prior to that, the police were not even aware that anything had been taken from the apartment.

Remarkably, when police began investigating Showery, they found his girlfriend in possession of Teresita's jewelry. Although the authorities declined to list the voice from beyond the grave as evidence, Showery was arrested, and he initially confessed to the crime. When his lawyers learned that information leading to his arrest had come from supernatural sources, they advised him to recant his confession.

## THE SURPRISE CONFESSION

Not surprisingly, the voice became a focal point of the case when it went to trial in January 1979. The defense called the Chuas to the witness stand in an effort to prove that the entire case against Showery was based on remarks made by a woman who claimed to be possessed—hardly the sort of evidence that would hold up in court.

But the prosecution argued that no matter the origin of the voice, it had turned out to be correct. In his closing remarks, prosecuting attorney Thomas Organ said, "Did Teresita Basa come back from the dead and name Showery? I don't know. I'm a skeptic, but it doesn't matter as to guilt or innocence. What does matter is that the information furnished to police checked out. The jewelry was found where the voice said it would be found, and Showery confessed."

Detective Stachula was asked if he believed the Chuas: "I would not call anyone a liar," he said. "...Dr. and Mrs. Chua are educated, intelligent people.... I listened and acted on what they told me...[and] the case was wrapped up within three hours."

Showery told the jury that he was "just kidding" when he confessed to the crime; he also claimed that the police had coerced him into an admission of guilt. Nevertheless, after 13 hours of deliberation, the jury reported that they were hopelessly deadlocked and a mistrial was declared.

A few weeks later, in a shocking development, Allan Showery changed his plea to "guilty" and was eventually sentenced to 14 years in prison. Some say that Teresita's ghost had visited him and frightened him into confessing.

Obviously shaken by the experience, the Chuas avoided the press as much as possible. In 1980, in her only interview with the press, Remibios noted that during the trial, people were afraid to ride in cars with her, but she said that she was never afraid because the voice said that God would protect her family. Still, she hoped that she would never have to go through such an experience again. "I've done my job," she said. "I don't think I will ever want to go through this same ordeal."

Having attracted national attention, the case quickly became the subject of a best-selling book and countless magazine articles, a TV movie, and a 1990 episode of *Unsolved Mysteries*. The case is often cited as "proof" of psychic phenomena, possession, and ghosts, but it's simply another mystery of the paranormal world. Exactly what it proves is impossible to say; after all, the ghost of Teresita Basa is no longer talking.

# POPPING HIS TOP: THE SEAFORD POLTERGEIST

Poltergeists are the publicity hounds of the spirit world. While other ghosts are content to appear in the shadows and then vanish so that nobody's ever exactly sure what they saw, poltergeist activities are always very flashy and conspicuous. Need furniture rearranged or doors opened or slammed shut? How about knickknacks moved around or plates smashed? If so, just call your neighborhood poltergeist; they love to perform such mischief in plain sight. Poltergeists don't care—they aren't part of the ghostly union. They just enjoy annoying (and scaring) the living.

## POP! POP! POP!

The science of investigating poltergeist activity has come a long way since the days when people blamed it all on witchcraft. One of the cases that got folks thinking that there might be more to it was the story of the Seaford Poltergeist.

This entity first made itself known to the Herrmann family of Seaford, Long Island, in early February 1958. Mrs. Herrmann had just welcomed her children Lucille and Jimmy home from school when several bottles in various rooms of the house all popped their tops and spewed their contents all over. The family considered various explanations, such as excess humidity or pressure building up in the bottles, but the tops were all of the twist-off variety. Short of a miniature tornado yanking the tops off, there seemed to be no rational explanation.

After the same thing happened several more times, Mr. Herrmann began to suspect that his son Jimmy—who had an interest in science—was somehow pulling a fast one on the family. However, after carefully watching the child while the incident happened, Herrmann knew that unless his son was a future Einstein, there was no way that the boy could be responsible. With no "ghost busters" to consult, Mr. Herrmann did the next best thing he could in 1958: He called the police.

Dubious at first, the police launched an investigation after witnessing some of the episodes firsthand. But answers were not forthcoming, and the incidents kept occurring. Even having a priest bless the house and sprinkle holy water in each of its rooms didn't help. An exorcism was considered but rejected because the incidents didn't resemble the work of a demon. Rather, they seemed to be the antics of a poltergeist (a noisy spirit).

## EXPLANATION UNKNOWN

Word of the events attracted the attention of the media as well as curiosity seekers. All explanations—from the scientifically sound (sonic booms, strong drafts, freakish magnetic waves) to the weird and wacky (Soviet satellite *Sputnik*)—were considered and dismissed. Although this was the Cold War era, it was unclear how tormenting a single American family fit into the Soviets' dastardly scheme of world domination.

What was far more worrisome was that the incidents seemed to be escalating in violence. Instead of just bottles popping open, objects such as a sugar bowl, a record player, and a heavy bookcase were tossed around. Fortunately, help soon arrived in the form of experts from Duke University's Parapsychology Laboratory. Their theory was that someone in the house was unwittingly moving objects via Recurrent Spontaneous Psychokinesis (RSPK). Children seemed to attract such activity, and the Duke team discovered that Jimmy had been at or near the scene of the incidents most of the time.

When one of the researchers spent time with the boy—playing cards, helping him with his homework, or just talking—the unusual activity declined. Two more incidents occurred in early March before the Seaford Poltergeist apparently packed its bags and moved on. After 67 recorded incidents in five weeks, the lives of the Herrmann family returned to normal. To this day, it is still unknown exactly what caused the strange events in the Herrmann household in early 1958.

# RESURRECTION MARY

Most big cities have their share of ghost stories, and Chicago is no different. But beyond the tales of haunted houses, spirit-infested graveyards, and spooky theaters, there is one Chicago legend that stands out among the rest. It's the story of a beautiful female phantom, a hitchhiking ghost that nearly everyone in the Windy City has heard of. Her name is "Resurrection Mary" and she is Chicago's most famous ghost.

## THE GIRL BY THE SIDE OF THE ROAD

The story of Resurrection Mary begins in the mid-1930s, when drivers began reporting a ghostly young woman on the road near the gates of Resurrection Cemetery, located on Archer Avenue in Chicago's southwestern suburbs. Some drivers claimed that she was looking for a ride, but others reported that she actually attempted to jump onto the running boards of their automobiles as they drove past.

A short time later, the reports took another, more mysterious turn. The unusual incidents moved away from the cemetery and began to center around the Oh Henry Ballroom (known today as Willowbrook Ballroom), located a few miles south of the graveyard on Archer Avenue. Many claimed to see the young woman on the road near the ballroom and sometimes inside the dance hall itself. Young men claimed that they met the girl at a dance, spent the evening with her, and then offered her a ride home at closing time. Her vague directions always led them north along Archer Avenue until they reached the gates of Resurrection Cemetery—where the girl would inexplicably vanish from the car.

Some drivers even claimed to accidentally run over the girl outside the cemetery. When they went to her aid, her body was always gone. Others said that their automobiles actually passed through the young woman before she disappeared through the cemetery gates.

Police and local newspapers began hearing similar stories from frightened and frazzled drivers who had encountered the mysterious young woman. These firsthand accounts created the legend of "Resurrection Mary," as she came to be known.

## WILL THE REAL RESURRECTION MARY PLEASE STAND UP?

One version of the story says that Resurrection Mary was a young woman who died on Archer Avenue in the early 1930s. On a cold winter's night, Mary spent the evening dancing at the Oh Henry Ballroom, but after an argument with her boyfriend, she decided to walk home. She was killed when a passing car slid on the ice and struck her.

According to the story, Mary was buried in Resurrection Cemetery, and since that time, she has been spotted along Archer Avenue. Many believe that she may be returning to her eternal resting place after one last dance.

This legend has been told countless times over the years and there may actually be some elements of truth to it— although, there may be more than one "Resurrection Mary" haunting Archer Avenue.

One of the prime candidates for Mary's real-life identity was a young Polish girl named Mary Bregovy. Mary loved to dance, especially at the Oh Henry Ballroom, and was killed one night in March 1934 after spending the evening at the ballroom and then downtown at some of the late-night clubs. She was killed along Wacker Drive in Chicago when the car that she was riding in collided with an elevated train support. Her parents buried her in Resurrection Cemetery, and then, a short time later, a cemetery caretaker spotted her ghost walking through the graveyard. Stranger still, passing motorists on Archer Avenue soon began telling stories of her apparition trying to hitch rides as they passed the cemetery's front gates. For this reason, many believe that the ghost stories of Mary Bregovy may have given birth to the legend of Resurrection Mary.

However, she may not be the only one. As encounters

with Mary have been passed along over the years, many descriptions of the phantom have varied. Mary Bregovy had bobbed, light-brown hair, but some reports describe Resurrection Mary as having long blonde hair. Who could this ghost be?

It's possible that this may be a young woman named Mary Miskowski, who was killed along Archer Avenue in October 1930. According to sources, she also loved to dance at the Oh Henry Ballroom and at some of the local nightspots. Many people who knew her in life believed that she might be the ghostly hitchhiker reported in the southwestern suburbs.

In the end, we may never know Resurrection Mary's true identity. But there's no denying that sightings of her have been backed up with credible eyewitness accounts. In these real, first-person reports, witnesses give specific places, dates, and times for their encounters with Mary—encounters that remain unexplained to this day. Besides that, Mary is one of the few ghosts to ever leave physical evidence behind!

## THE GATES OF RESURRECTION CEMETERY

On August 10, 1976, around 10:30 P.M., a man driving past Resurrection Cemetery noticed a young girl wearing a white dress standing inside the cemetery gates. She was holding on to the bars of the gate, looking out toward the road. Thinking that she was locked in the cemetery, the man stopped at a nearby police station and alerted an officer to the young woman's predicament. An officer responded to the call, but when he arrived at the cemetery, the girl was gone. He called out with his loudspeaker and looked for her with his spotlight, but nobody was there. However, when he walked up to the gates for a closer inspection, he saw something very unusual. It looked as though someone had pulled two of the green-colored bronze bars with such intensity that handprints were seared into the metal. The bars were blackened and burned at precisely the spot where a small woman's hands would have been.

When word got out about the handprints, people from all over the area came to see them. Cemetery officials denied that anything supernatural had occurred, and they later claimed that the marks were created when a truck accidentally backed into the gates and a workman had tried to heat them up and bend them back. It was a convenient explanation but one that failed to explain the indentations that appeared to be left by small fingers and were plainly visible in the metal.

Cemetery officials were disturbed by this new publicity, so, in an attempt to dispel the crowds of curiosity-seekers, they tried to remove the marks with a blowtorch. However, this made them even more noticeable, so they cut out the bars with plans to straighten or replace them.

But removing the bars only made things worse as people wondered what the cemetery had to hide. Local officials were so embarrassed that the bars were put back into place, straightened, and then left alone so that the burned areas would oxidize and eventually match the other bars. However, the blackened areas of the bars did not oxidize, and the twisted handprints remained obvious until the late 1990s when the bars were finally removed. At great expense, Resurrection Cemetery replaced the entire front gates and the notorious bars were gone for good.

## A BROKEN SPIRIT LINGERS ON

Sightings of Resurrection Mary aren't as frequent as in years past, but they do still continue. Even though a good portion of the encounters can be explained by the fact that Mary has become such a part of Chicago lore that nearly everyone has heard of her, some of the sightings seem to be authentic. So whether you believe in her or not, Mary is still seen walking along Archer Avenue, people still claim to pick her up during the cold winter months, and she continues to be the Windy City's most famous ghost.

# A SUPERIOR HAUNTING: THE EDMUND FITZGERALD

Many ships have been lost to the dangers of the Great Lakes, but few incidents have fascinated the world like the sinking of the *Edmund Fitzgerald* off the shores of northern Michigan on November 10, 1975. The mysterious circumstances of the tragedy, which took 29 lives, and lingering tales of a haunting—all memorialized in a 1976 song by Gordon Lightfoot—have kept the horrific story fresh for more than three decades.

## LEAST LIKELY TO SINK

Lake Superior is well known among sailors for its treachery, especially when the unusually strong autumn winds sailors call the "Witch of November" roil the waves. But the 729-foot-long *Edmund Fitzgerald* was considered as unsinkable as any steamer ever launched, and its cost of $8.4 million made it the most expensive freighter in history at the time.

At its christening in June 1958, it was the Great Lakes' largest freighter, built with state-of-the-art technology, comfortable crew quarters, and elegant staterooms for guests. Its name honored Edmund Fitzgerald, the son of a sea captain and the president of Northwestern Mutual

Insurance Company, who had commissioned the boat.

During the christening, a few incidents occurred that some saw as bad omens from the get-go. As a crowd of more than 10,000 watched, it took Mrs. Fitzgerald three tries to shatter the bottle of champagne. Then, when the ship was released into the water, it hit the surface at the wrong angle and kicked up a wave that splattered the entire ceremonial area with lake water, and knocked the ship into a nearby dock. If that weren't enough, one spectator died on the spot of a heart attack.

## THE LAST LAUNCH

The weather was unseasonably pleasant the morning of November 9, 1975, so much so that the crew of 29 men who set sail from Superior, Wisconsin, that day were unlikely to have been concerned about their routine trip to Zug Island on the Detroit River. But the captain, Ernest McSorley, knew a storm was in the forecast.

McSorley was a 44-year veteran of the lakes, had captained the *Fitzgerald* since 1972, and was thought to have been planning his retirement for the following year. He paid close attention to the gale warnings issued that afternoon, but no one suspected they would turn into what weather-watchers called a "once in a lifetime storm." However, when the weather report was upgraded to a full storm warning, McSorley changed course to follow a route safer than the normal shipping lanes, instead chugging closer to the Canadian shore.

Following the *Fitzgerald* in a sort of "buddy" system was another freighter, the *Arthur Anderson*. The two captains stayed in contact as they traveled together through winds measuring up to 50 knots (about 58 miles per hour) with waves splashing 12 feet or higher. Around 1:00 P.M., McSorley advised Captain Cooper of the *Anderson* that the *Fitzgerald* was "rolling." By about 2:45 P.M., as the *Anderson* moved to avoid a dangerous shoal near Caribou Island, a crewman sighted the *Fitzgerald* about 16 miles ahead, closer to the shoal than Cooper thought safe.

About 3:30 P.M., McSorley reported to Cooper that the *Fitzgerald* had sustained some minor damage and was beginning to list, or roll to one side. The ships were still 16–17 miles apart. At 4:10 P.M., with waves now lashing 18 feet high, McSorley radioed that his ship had lost radar capability. The two ships stayed in radio contact until about 7:00 P.M. when the *Fitzgerald* crew told the *Anderson* they were "holding [their] own." After that, radio contact was lost and the *Fitzgerald* dropped off the radar. Around 8:30 P.M., Cooper told the coast guard at Sault Ste. Marie that the *Fitzgerald* appeared to be missing. The search was on.

Evidently, the *Fitzgerald* sank sometime after 7:10 P.M. on November 10, just 17 miles from the shore of Whitefish Point, Michigan. Despite a massive search effort, it wasn't until November 14 that a navy flyer detected a magnetic anomaly that turned out to be the wreck of the *Fitzgerald*. The only other evidence of the disaster to surface was a handful of lifeboats, life jackets, and some oars, tools, and propane tanks. A robotic vehicle was used to thoroughly photograph the wreck in May 1976.

## ONE MYSTERIOUS BODY

One troubling aspect of the *Fitzgerald* tragedy was that no bodies were found. In most lakes or temperate waters, corpses rise to the surface as decomposition causes gases to form, which makes bodies float. But the Great Lakes are so cold that decomposition and the formation of these gases is inhibited, causing bodies to remain on the lake bottom. One explanation was that the crew had been contained in the ship's enclosed areas. The wildest speculation surmised that a UFO destroyed the ship and aliens abducted the men.

In 1994, a Michigan businessman named Frederick Shannon took a tugboat and a 16-foot submarine equipped with a full array of modern surveillance equipment to the site, hoping to produce a documentary about the ship. But his crew was surprised when they discovered a body near the bow of the wreck, which had settled into the lake bottom. The remains were covered by cork sections of a deteriorated canvas life vest and were photographed but not retrieved. However, there was nothing to conclusively prove that this body was associated with the *Fitzgerald*. Two French vessels were lost in the same region in 1918, and none of those bodies had been recovered either. A sailor lost from one of them could have been preserved by the lake's frigid water and heavy pressure.

Many have pondered whether the men of the *Edmund Fitzgerald* might have been saved had they had better disaster equipment, but survival time in such cold water is only minutes. Most of the life jackets later floated to the surface, indicating that the crewmen never put them on. The waters were much too rough to launch wooden lifeboats, and there was probably no time to find and inflate rubber life rafts.

## WHAT SANK THE MIGHTY FITZ?

She went down fast—that much was evident. Three different organizations filed official reports on the ship's sinking without coming to any common conclusions. It was thought impossible for such a large, well-built, and relatively "young" ship, only in its 18th year, to break up and sink so quickly, particularly in this age of modern navigation and communication equipment.

One popular theory is that the *Fitzgerald* ventured too close to the dangerous Six-Fathom Shoal near Caribou Island and scraped over it, damaging the hull. Another is that the ship's hatch covers were either faulty or improperly clamped, which allowed water infiltration. Wave height may also have played its part, with the storm producing a series of gargantuan swells known as the "Three Sisters"—a trio of lightning-fast waves that pound a vessel with a 1–2–3 punch—the first washes over the deck, the second hits the deck again so fast that the first has not had time to clear itself, and the third quickly adds another heavy wash, piling thousands of gallons of water on the ship at once. Few ships have the ability to remain afloat under such an onslaught.

In addition, the ship was about 200 feet longer than the 530-feet-deep water where it floundered. If the waves pushed the ship bow-first down into the water, it would have hit bottom and stuck (which is what appears to have happened), snapping the long midsection in two as a result of continuing wave action and exploding steam boilers. The ship's 26,000-pound cargo of iron ore pellets shifted as the ship twisted and sank, adding to the devastation.

Some fingers pointed to the ship's prior damages. The *Fitzgerald* had been knocked around a bit during its career on the lakes: In 1969, it crunched ground near the locks at Sault Ste. Marie, Michigan, and less than a year later, in April 1970, it sustained a minor collision with the S.S. *Hochelaga*. In September of that year, the *Fitzgerald* slammed a lock wall for a total of three damaging hits within the span of 12 months. It's possible that these impacts inflicted more structural problems than were realized or that they were not repaired properly.

## SPIRITS OF THE LAKE

Author Hugh E. Bishop says that since the mighty *Fitz* went down, sailors have claimed to see a ghostly ship in the vicinity of the sinking. The captain of a coast guard cutter, the *Woodrush*, was on duty near the *Fitzgerald* site in 1976 and spent a night stuck in shifting ice masses directly over the wreckage. All throughout the night, the captain's normally carefree black Labrador whined and cowered, avoiding certain spots on the ship as if some invisible presence existed.

Bishop also noted that on October 21, 1975, a San Antonio psychic named J. Nickie Jackson recorded in her diary a dream she'd had that foretold the *Fitzgerald*'s doom. In her dream, she saw the freighter struggling to stay afloat in giant waves before it finally plunged straight down into the depths. The real-life event occurred just three weeks later. Jackson was familiar with the *Edmund Fitzgerald* because she had previously lived in Superior but was surprised to dream about it in her new life in Texas.

## FOR WHOM THE BELL TOLLS...

On July 4, 1995, a year after the lone body was documented, the bell of the *Edmund Fitzgerald* was retrieved from the wreckage and laid to rest in the Great Lakes Shipwreck Historical Museum in Whitefish Bay, Michigan. With the wreckage, the diving crew left a replica of the bell, which symbolizes the ship's "spirit." Every year on November 10, during a memorial service, the original, 200-pound, bronze bell is now rung 29 times—once for each crewmember that perished on the *Edmund Fitzgerald*.

# THE WATSEKA WONDER:
# A TALE OF POSSESSION

Spiritual possession—in which a person's body is taken over by the spirit of another—is easy to fake, and legitimate cases are incredibly rare. One of the most widely publicized possessions occurred in Watseka, Illinois, in the late 1870s, when the spirit of Mary Roff, a girl who had died 12 years earlier, inhabited the body of 13-year-old Lurancy Vennum. This astounding case became known as the "Watseka Wonder."

In 1865, Mary Roff was just 18 years old when she died in an insane asylum following a lifelong illness that tormented her with frequent fits, seizures, and strange voices in her head. She'd also developed an obsession with bloodletting and would apply leeches to her body, poke herself with pins, and cut herself with razors. Doctors thought that Mary was mentally ill, but others—including her own family—came to believe that her problems were supernatural in origin.

At the time of Mary Roff's death, Lurancy Vennum was barely a year old. Born on April 16, 1864, Lurancy moved with her family to Watseka a few years after Mary Roff's death and knew nothing of the girl or her family.

In July 1877, about 12 years after Mary passed away, Lurancy started to exhibit symptoms similar to Mary's, including uncontrollable seizures. Her speech became garbled, and she often spoke in a strange language. She sometimes fell into trances, assumed different personalities, and claimed to see spirits, many of which terrified her.

The townspeople of Watseka didn't know what to make of Lurancy. Many thought that she was insane and should be committed, as Mary had been. But the Roffs, who had become ardent Spiritualists as a result of their daughter's troubles, believed that unseen forces were tormenting Lurancy. They felt that she was not insane but rather was possessed by the spirits of the dead. With the permission of Lurancy's parents, Asa Roff—Mary's father—met with the young girl in the company of Dr. E. Winchester Stevens, who was also a Spiritualist. During their visit, a friendly spirit spoke to Lurancy and asked to take control of her body to protect her from sinister forces. That spirit was Mary Roff.

## SENT TO HEAVEN

After Mary took possession of Lurancy's body, she explained that Lurancy was ill and needed to return to heaven to be cured. Mary said that she would remain in Lurancy's body until sometime in May. Over the next few months, it seemed apparent that Mary's spirit was indeed in control of Lurancy's body. She looked the same, but she knew nothing about the Vennum family or her life as Lurancy. Instead, she had intimate knowledge of the Roffs, and she acted as though they were her family. Although she treated the Vennums politely, they were essentially strangers to her.

In February 1878, Lurancy/Mary asked to go live with her parents—the Roffs. The Vennums reluctantly consented. On the way to the Roff home, as they traveled past the house where they'd lived when Mary was alive, Lurancy wanted to know why they weren't stopping. The Roffs explained that they'd moved to a new home a few years back, which was something that Lurancy/Mary would not have known. Lurancy/Mary spent several months living in the Roff home, where she identified objects and people that Lurancy could not have known.

On one occasion, Lurancy sat down at the Roff's family piano and began to play, singing the same songs Mary had sung in her youth. One member of the Roff family commented, "As we stood listening, the familiar [songs] were hers, though emanating from another's lips."

Once word spread of Lurancy's spiritual possession, interested people started to visit. Lurancy/Mary typically met them in the Roffs' front parlor, where she frequently demonstrated knowledge of events that had transpired long before Lurancy was even born.

During one encounter with a Mrs. Sherman, Mary was asked about the people she had met in the afterlife. Immediately, Mary started listing the names of some of Mrs. Sherman's deceased family members, as well as several of Mrs. Sherman's neighbors who had died. Again, this was information that Lurancy could not possibly have known.

## SCENE AT A SÉANCE

In April 1878, during a séance that was held in the Roff home and attended by several people (including Dr. Stevens), one member of the group became possessed by the spirit of another member's dead brother, who addressed the gathering. After the spirit had left the man's body, Mary removed herself from Lurancy's body (which immediately lolled over against the person next to her, as if dead) and possessed the body of a participant named Dr. Steel. Through him, Mary proved to everyone present that it was indeed her. She then abandoned Dr. Steel's body and reentered Lurancy's.

## GOING HOME

Mary permanently left Lurancy's body on May 21, 1878. When Lurancy awoke from her trance, she was no longer afflicted by the numerous problems that had previously plagued her, nor did she have any recollection of being spiritually possessed by Mary. By all accounts, she came away from the experience a healthy young lady. Indeed, Lurancy grew to be a happy woman and exhibited no ill effects from the possession. She went on to marry and have 13 children.

But Mary didn't abandon Lurancy completely. According to some sources, Lurancy kept in touch with the Roff family, with whom she felt a strange closeness, although she had no idea why. She would visit with them once a year and allow Mary's spirit to possess her briefly, just like it did in the late 1870s.

The story of the Watseka Wonder still stands as one of the most authentic cases of spirit possession in history. It has been investigated, dissected, and ridiculed, but to this day, no clear scientific explanation has ever been offered.